love is...

...a wild ride

Kim Casali

HARRY N. ABRAMS, INC., PUBLISHERS

love is...

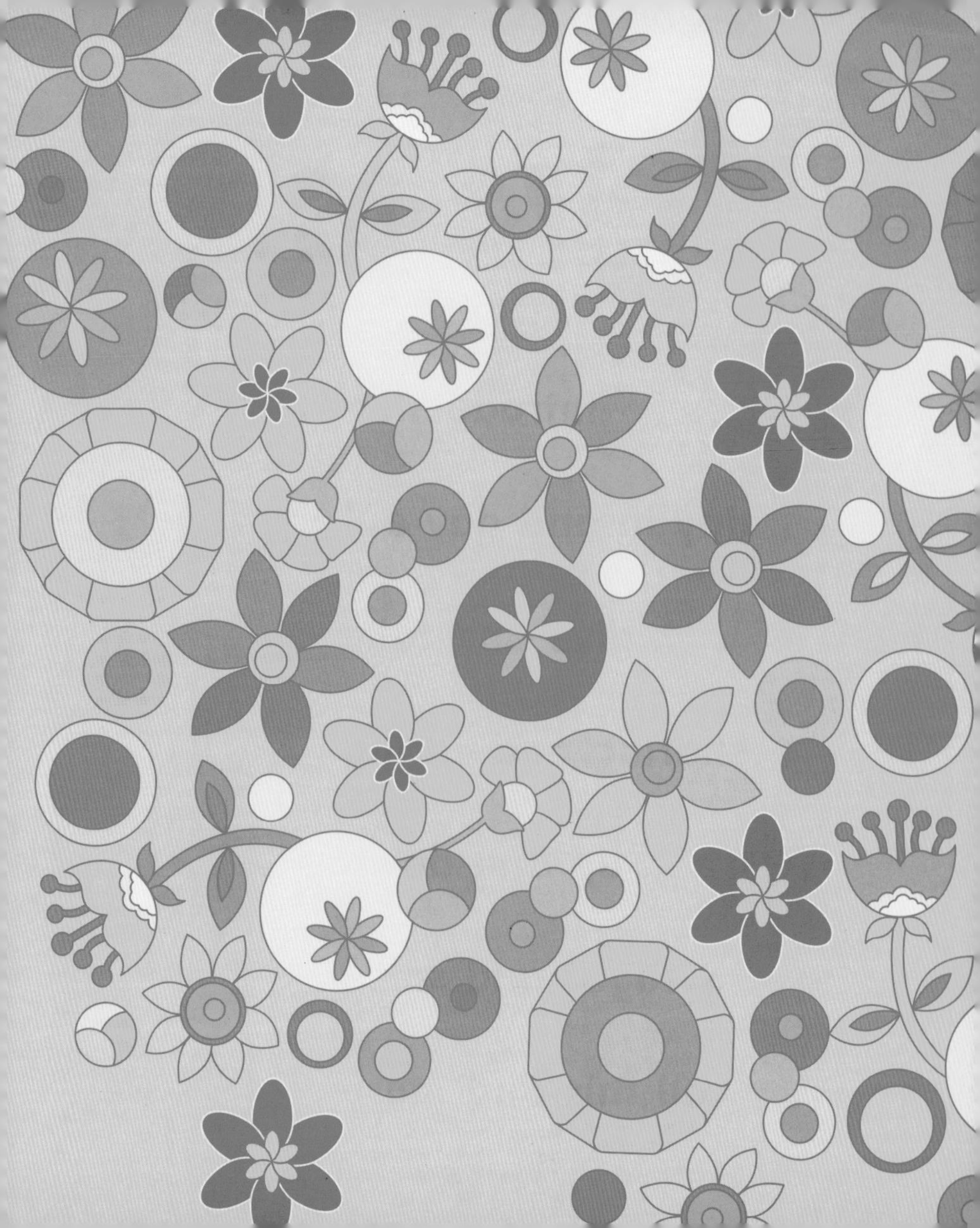

love is...

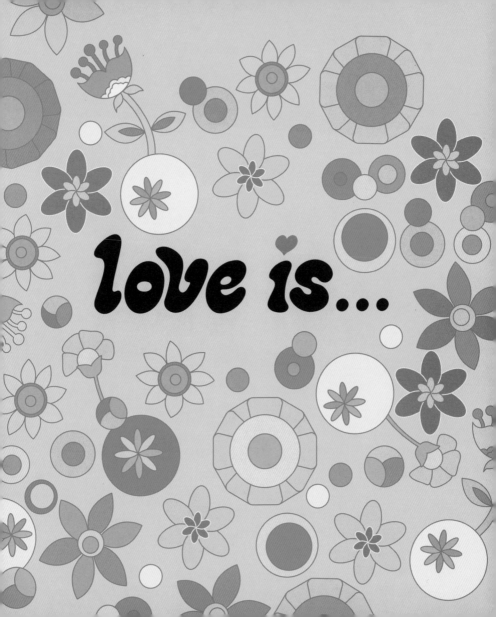

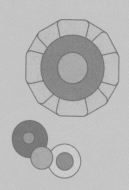

Introduction

The Love Is… phenomenon—endearing cartoons that bring smiles to the faces of everyone who sees them—began in the 1960s in the heart of artist Kim Casali. Shy by nature, Kim created these little "love notes" to express her feelings for a man named Roberto, the man she would eventually marry. She left her sweet drawings for him everywhere, in the pocket of his jeans, under his pillow, on the seat of his car, even in his sock drawer. Unbeknownst to her, Roberto kept each and every one of them. Believing his wife's drawings to be something very special, he decided to show them to someone in the syndication business who agreed that their heartfelt message should be made public. The first Love Is… cartoon was published in the *Los Angeles Times* on January 5, 1970, where it's appeared ever since.

Now, thirty-five years later, Love Is… remains as fresh and relevant as ever. A fixture in popular culture, its simple yet universal themes appeal to all generations: Love Is… intense, passionate, and exciting. Love Is… also stressful, frustrating, and even heartbreaking. Love Is… expressed day in and day out, in the little things: a cup of coffee in the morning, a back rub at night. And it is expressed in the big things: the birth of a child, the celebration of a life spent together. Love Is… something that starts with two people. It is what makes every day a special day. Love Is… all this and more.

Right: The first drawing, published on January 5, 1970, in the *Los Angeles Times*

love is...

...not picking the most expensive dish on the menu

love is...

. . . day in
and day out

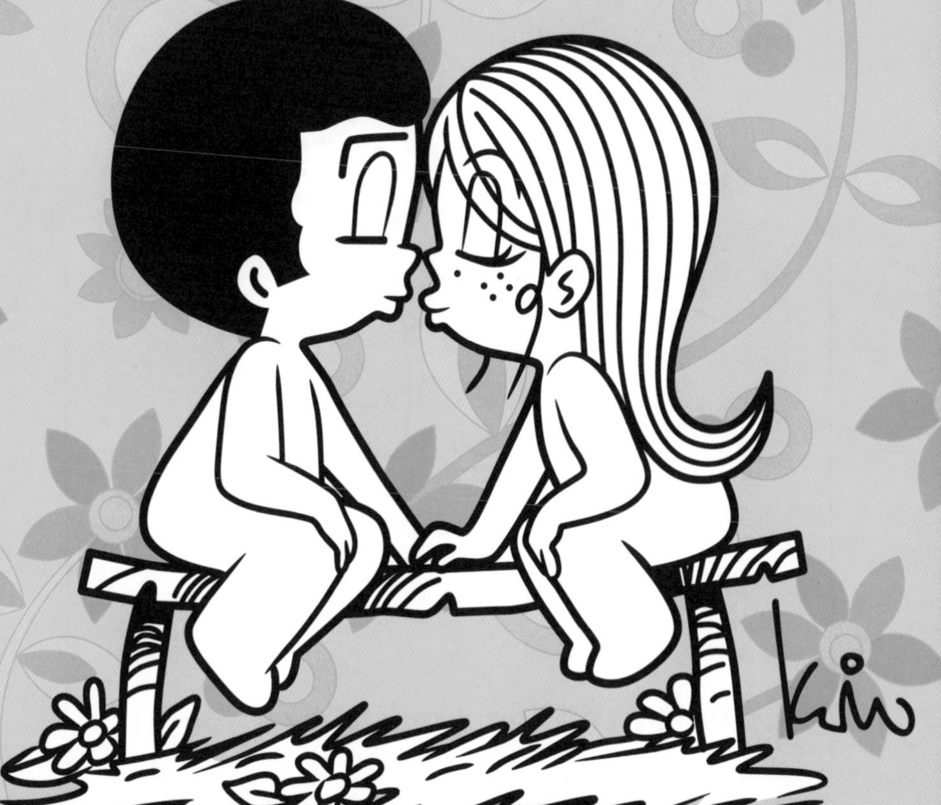

love is...

...what makes each day special

love is...

...telling her she's beautiful
in the morning

love is...

...picking up after yourself

love is...

...smiling at each other often

love is...

...winking at her over the morning paper

love is...

...returning his car with a full tank

love is...

...being the first thought that pops into his head

love is...

...getting the tangles out
of her hair

love is...

...secretly altering your schedule so that you can meet

love is...

...having his picture on
your desk

love is...

...breakfast in bed on Saturday morning

love is...

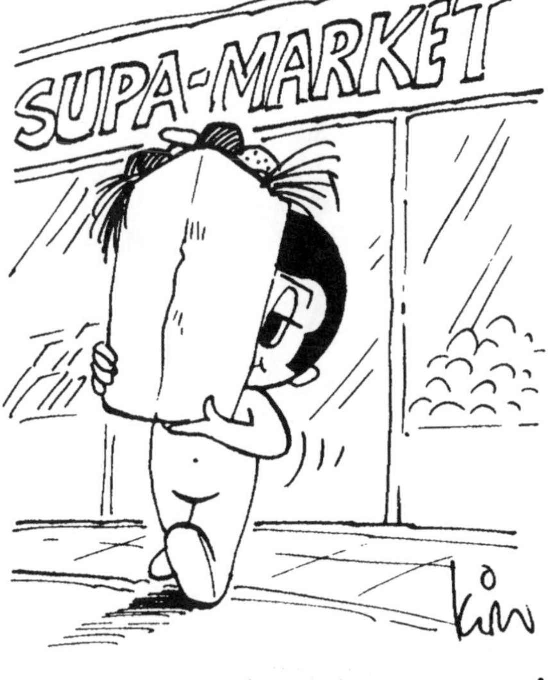
SUPA-MARKET
kim

...doing the supermarket shopping on your way home from work

love is...

...having a good mixer

love is...

...someone who makes
great pasta

love is...

...shopping together on Saturday

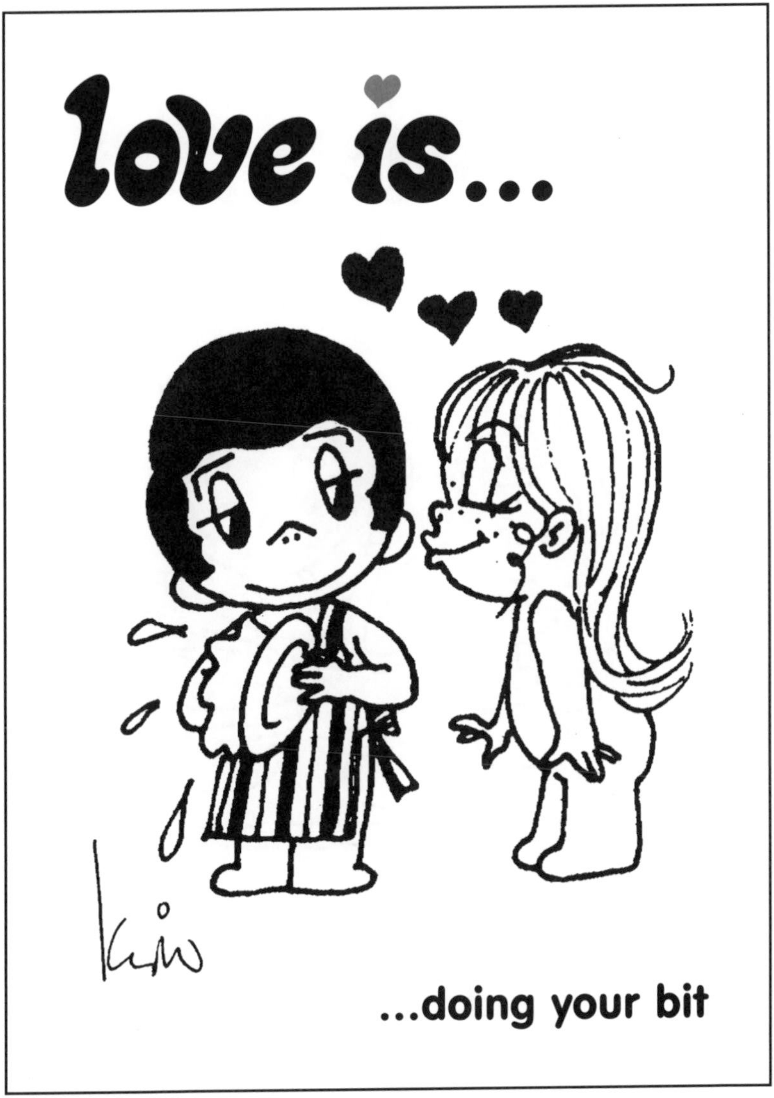
love is...
...doing your bit

love is...

...making bread together

love is...

...doing the dreary chores together

...putting up with his singing in the shower

love is...

...when he takes your picture
on his business trip

love is...

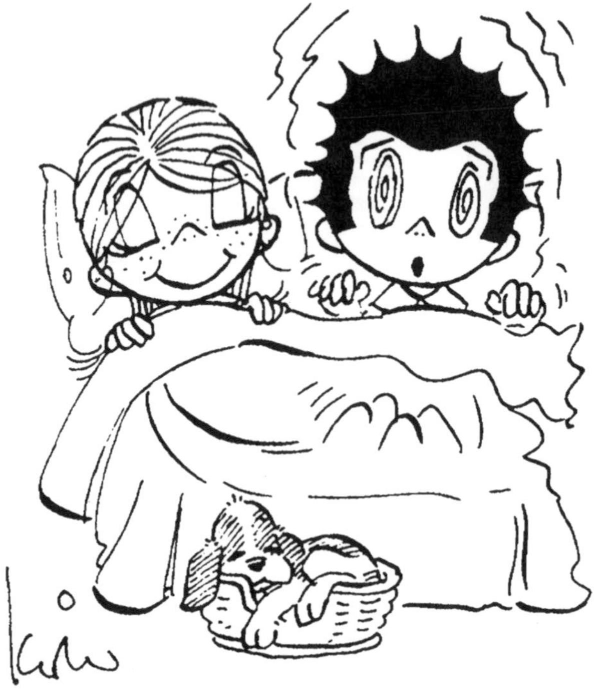

...when "cold feet" are a cure for snoring

...spelling "I love you"
in Scrabble

love is...

...trying to get the hang of
hanging paper

love is...

...double the fun when you're together

love is...

...hurrying to get home because you know he'll be there

love is...

...giving him a back rub after a long day

love is...

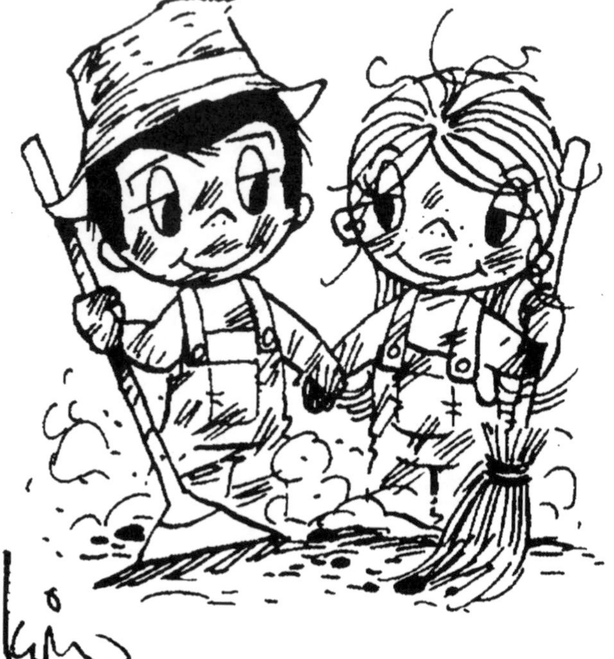

...being partners in grime

...stopping his snores with
a kiss

love is...

...someone who cooks and cleans for you

love is...

...when he does his share of
the housework

love is...

...forgetting the dishes every
once in a while

love is...

...secretly filling her tank

love is...

...sharing your wrinkle
prevention cream

love is...

...phoning when you're
running late

...waiting up when he's
working overtime

love is...

...spreading some real butter
on his croissant

love is...

...letting her take over the bathroom

love is...

...not fighting over who gets
the front page first

love is...

...a message on the mirror

love is...

...helping her hang her new picture

...someone to push your
supermarket cart

love is...

...doing things around the house

love is...

...making sure she takes
her vitamins

love is...

...being a good neighbor

love is...

...sending her a "smooch"
from your cell phone

love is...

...calmly going through the monthly bills together

love is...

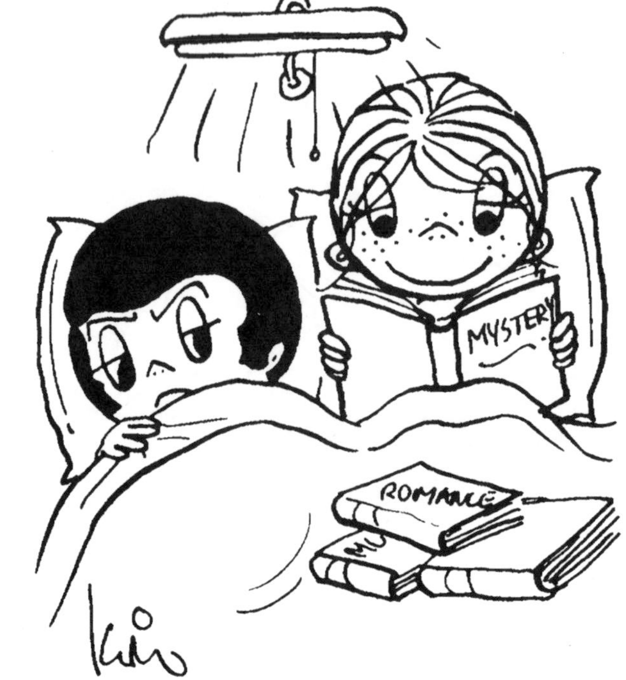
MYSTERY
ROMANCE

...not reading in bed for hours

love is...

...what makes every day
worth living

love is...

...waiting for him

love is...

...sticking a heart on his
bumper

love is...

...bringing her a pillow

...making the most of a
traffic jam

love is...

...snuggling up together

...having someone to bless you

love is...

...giving her the pick
of the bunch

love is...

...someone without too many strings attached

love is...

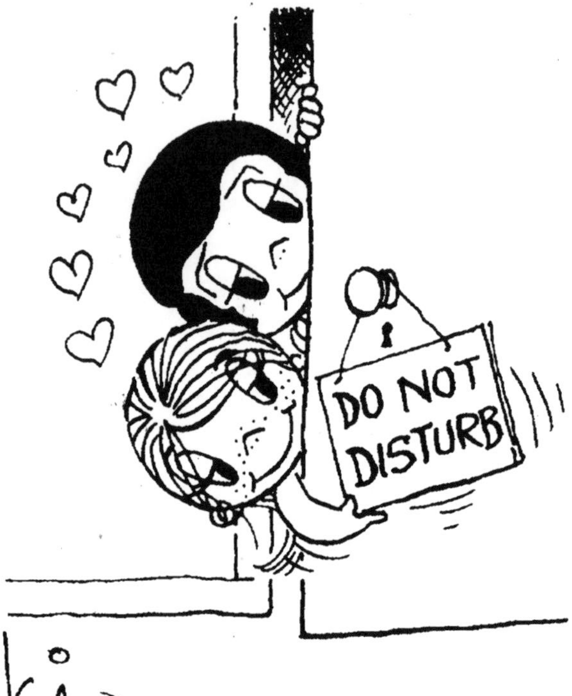
DO NOT
DISTURB

...making time to be together

love is...

...giving thanks for every day
you've known each other

love is...

...a regular bouquet of flowers

love is...

...helping with the homework

love is...

...like blasting off

love is...

...bringing in the harvest
together

love is...

...not minding if you catch
his cold

love is...

...when time drags on your own

love is...

...a rose through your
letter slot

love is...

...playing her favorite tunes in the car

love is...

...wearing the dress he likes

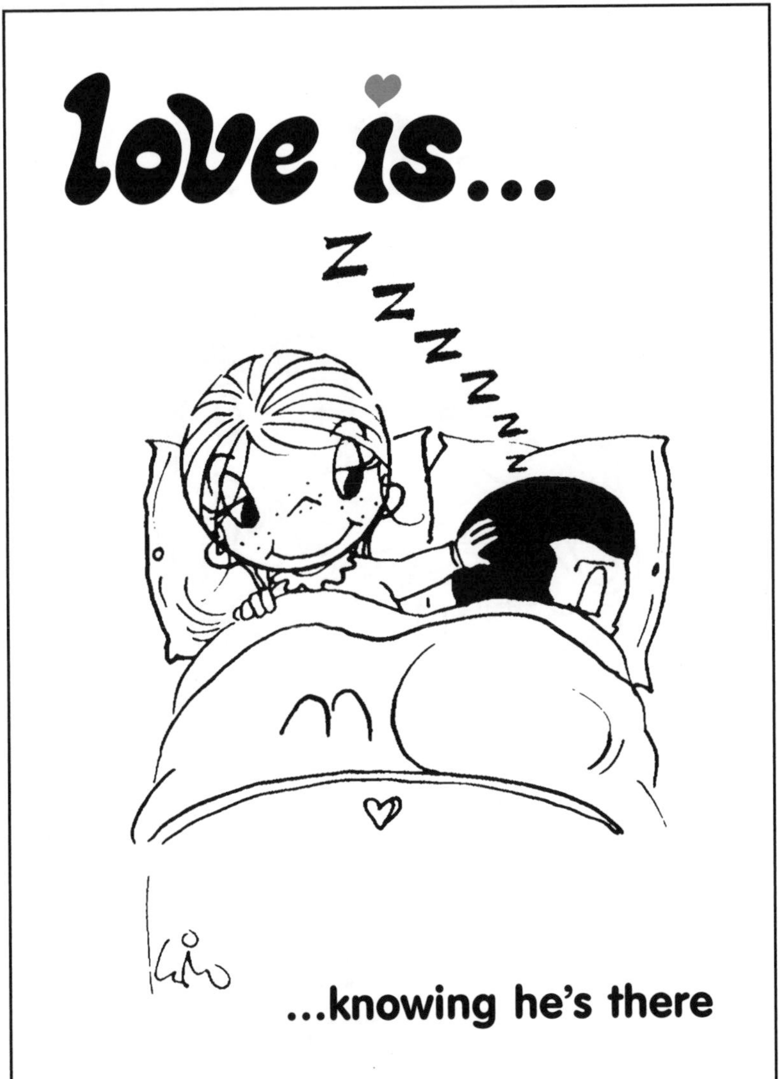
love is...

...knowing he's there

love is...

...a lunch date that lasts
through dinner

love is...

...what gives you something to whistle about

love is...

...not making so many demands

love is...

...two mugs together

...turning the other cheek

love is...

...a phone call to chase away
your blues

love is...

...when your heart skips a beat

love is...

...holding hands

...when your heart sinks to your boots during an argument

love is...

...asking her if she likes your aftershave

love is...

...knowing that chivalry is
not dead

...finding a note on the fridge
when you get home

love is...

...paying him a compliment

love is...

...putting your heads together

love is...

...when he's your first and
last thought of the day

love is...

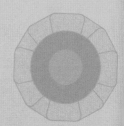

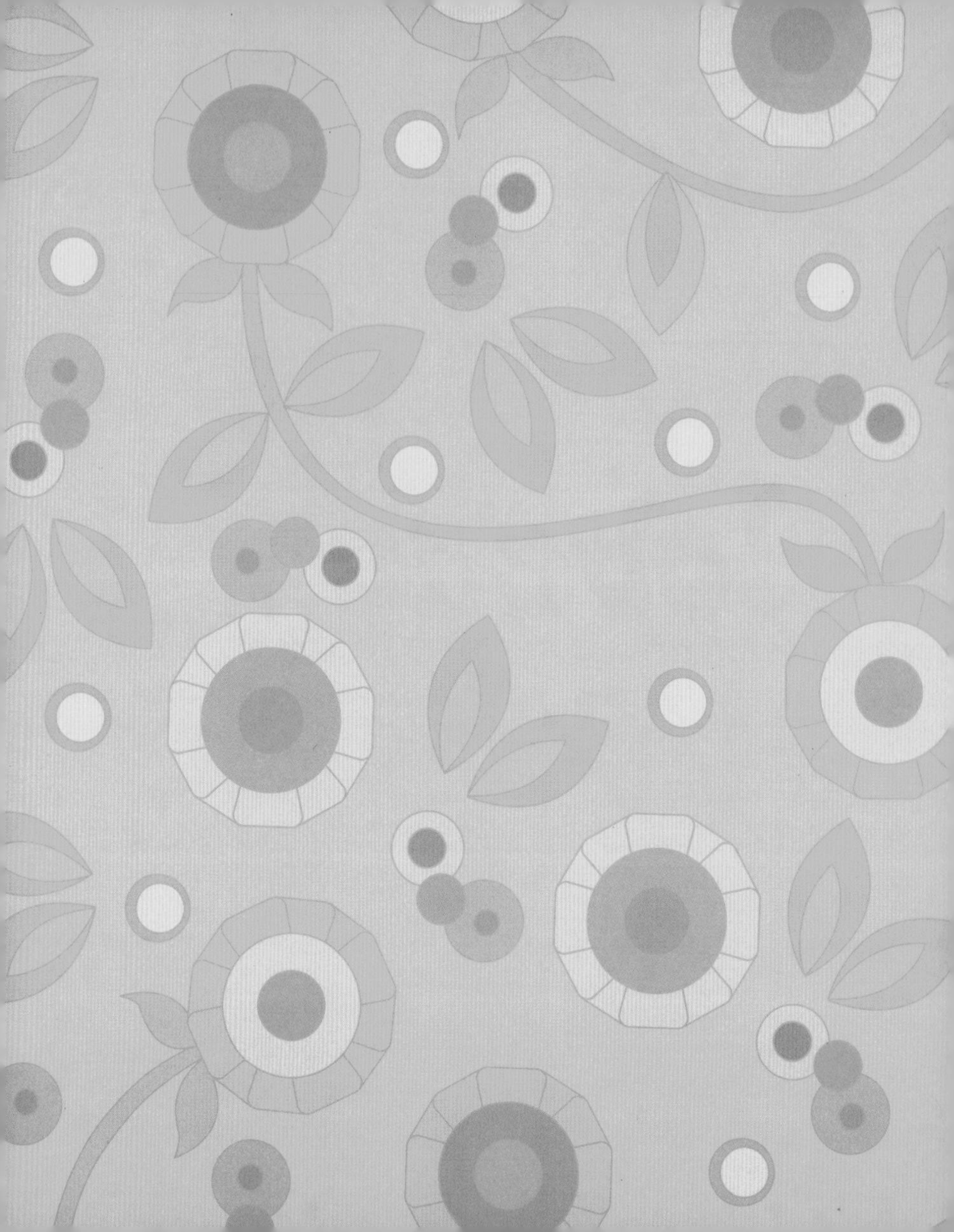

...give and take

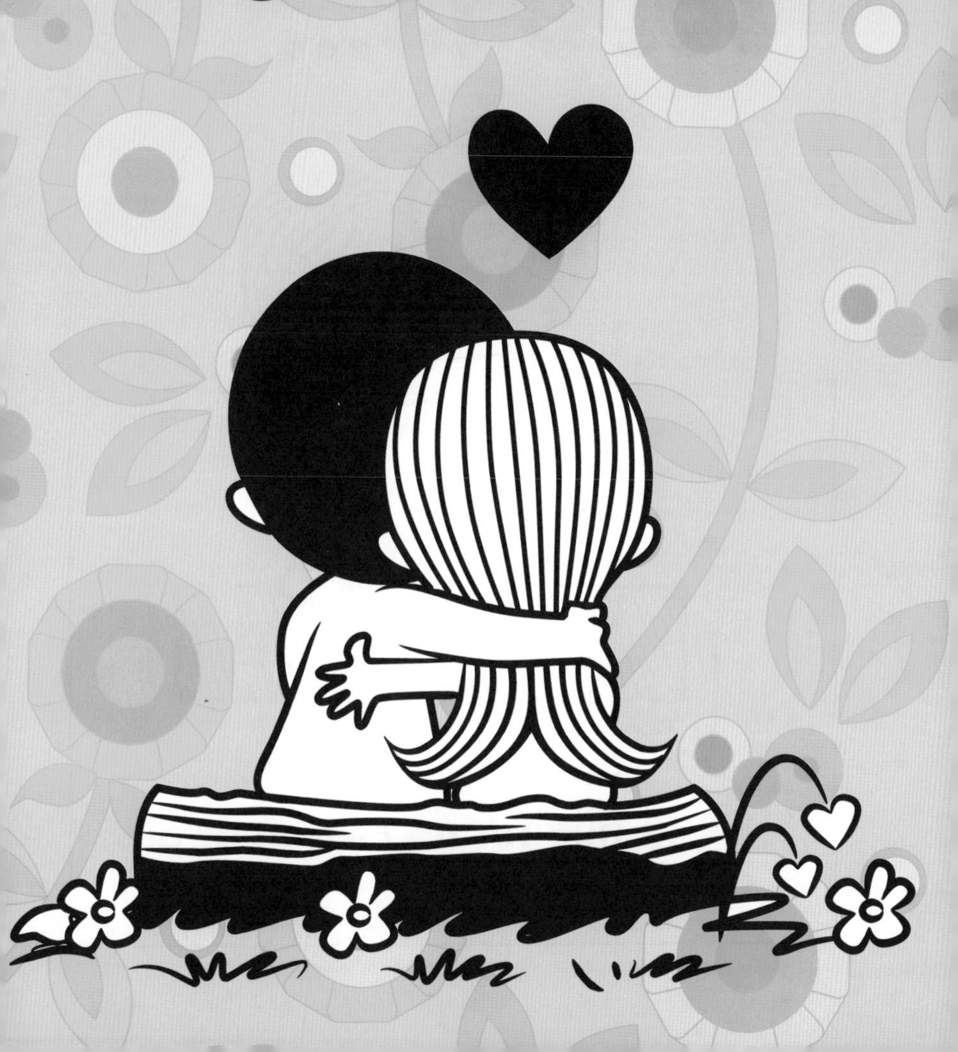

love is...

...a hug for no reason at all

...babysitting so that she can go out sometimes

love is...

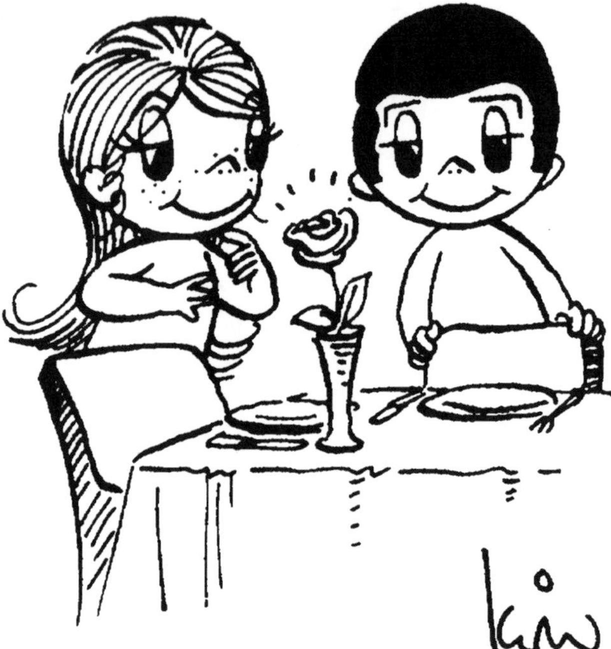

...the little things

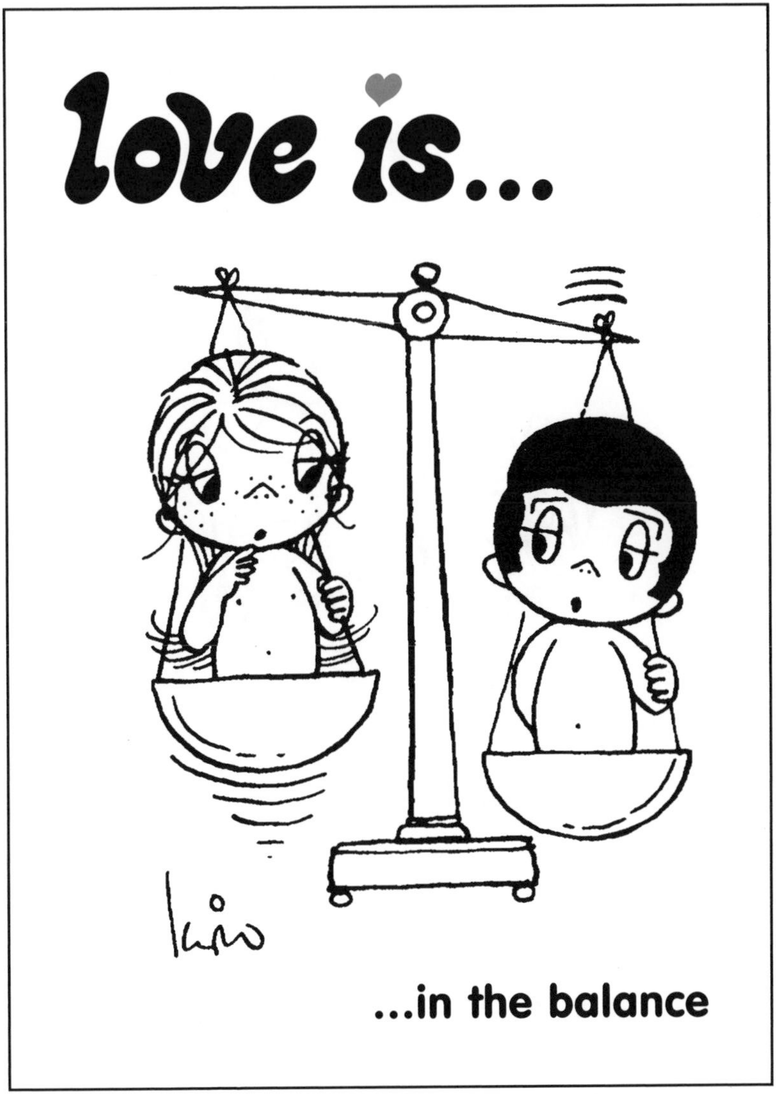
love is...
...in the balance

love is...

...having someone to shop for

...going shopping with her

love is...

**...some of the little things
he does**

love is...

...a dozen red roses

love is...

...an unexpected gift

love is...

...payment in kind

love is...

...just for you

love is...

...guessing who's behind it

love is...

...brightening up his
Monday with a call

love is...

...giving 'til it hurts

...when everything's "ours,"
not his and hers

love is...

...a gentle hand to help you

love is...

...bringing a "peace offering"

love is...

...making her favorite nightcap

love is...

...offering her the last cookie

love is...

...giving her a present just
because

love is...

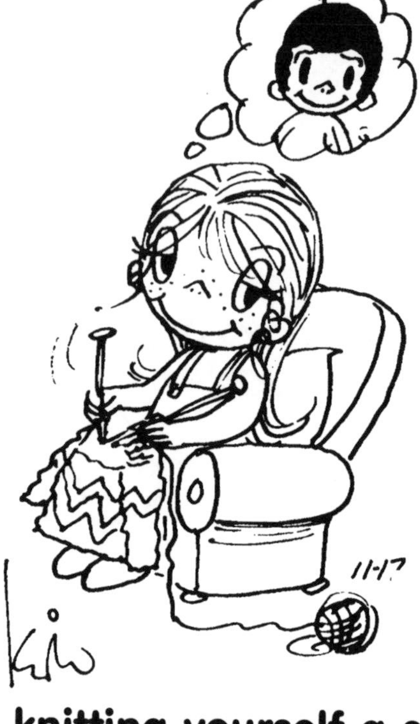

...knitting yourself a sweater in his favorite color

love is...

...when he sends you
a love note

love is...

...giving him your last dollar

love is...

...sharing an order of French fries

love is...

...giving him an "unbirthday" present

...the very best you can give

love is...

...remembering to give as well
as take affection

love is...

...a chocolate birthday cake

love is...

...when you both take the
back seat

love is...

...being the dog walker when the weather's bad

love is...

...shelling pistachios for him

love is...

...giving him healthy meals

...not expecting a three-course meal every night

love is...

...thinking of what he would like for his birthday

love is...

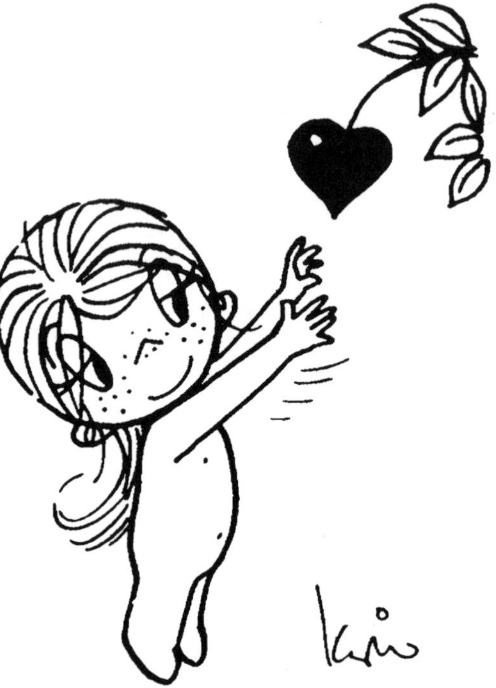

...there for the taking

love is...

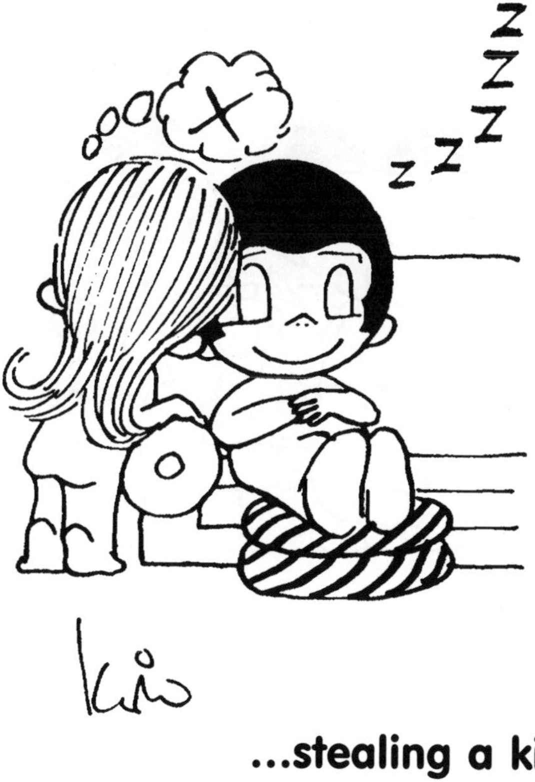
z z Z Z Z Z

...stealing a kiss

love is...

...sometimes being a
good listener

love is...

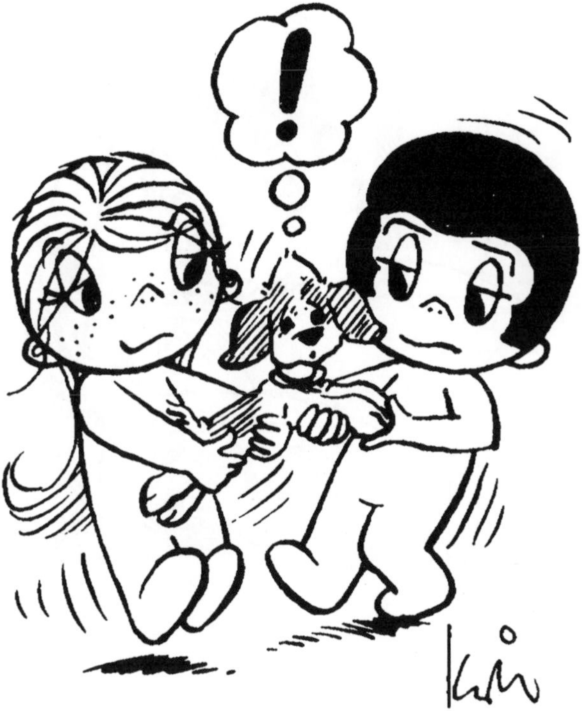
!
Kim

...sometimes a tug-of-war

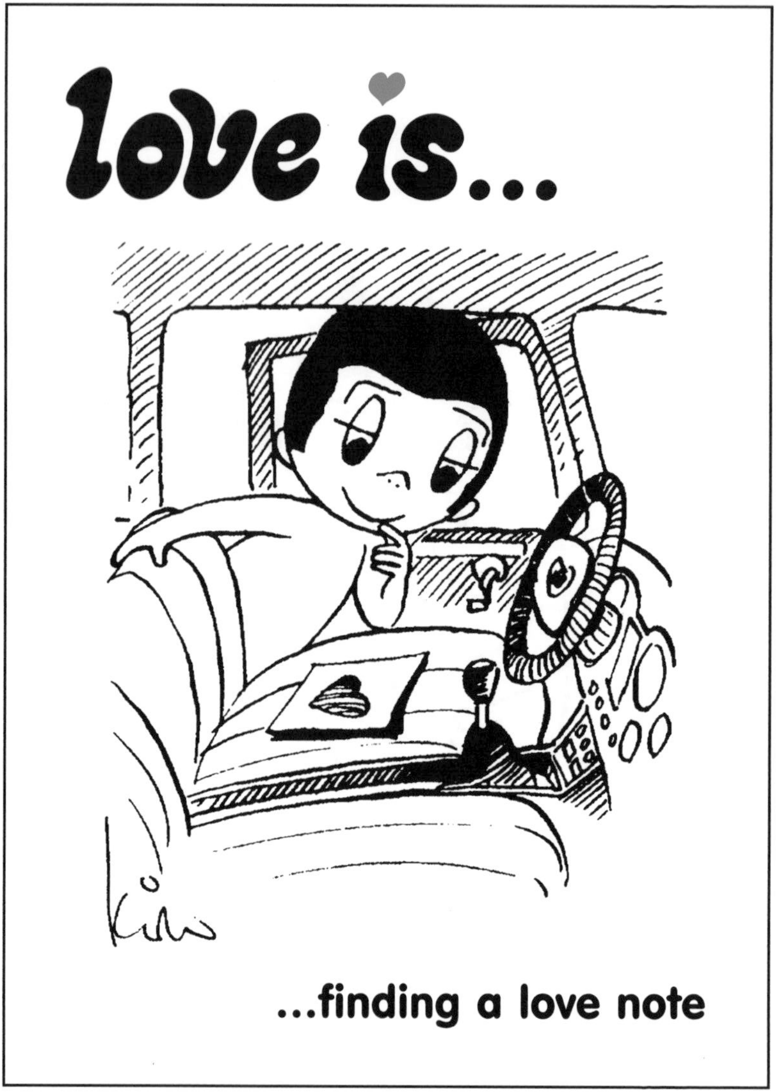
love is...
...finding a love note

love is...

...searching for a four-leaf clover for him

love is...

...faxing him kisses

love is...

...looking after her dog when she's away

love is...

...inviting him over for dinner

love is...

...doing little things for her

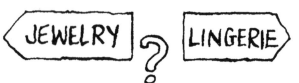

...trying to think of an original gift

love is...

...two people sharing one heart

love is...

...stopping to buy flowers on your way home

love is...

...saying plenty of "pleases"
and "thank yous"

love is...

...a little give and take

love is...

...remembering her birthday

love is...

...wanting to give her the moon and the stars

love is...

...giving your little brother
a hug

love is...

...sometimes doing things
he likes

love is...

...returning his kiss

love is...

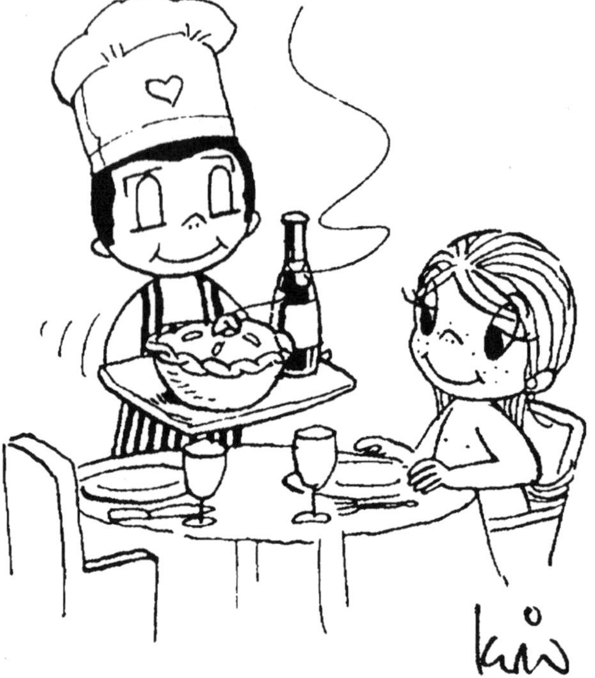

...surprising her

love is...

. . sharing and caring

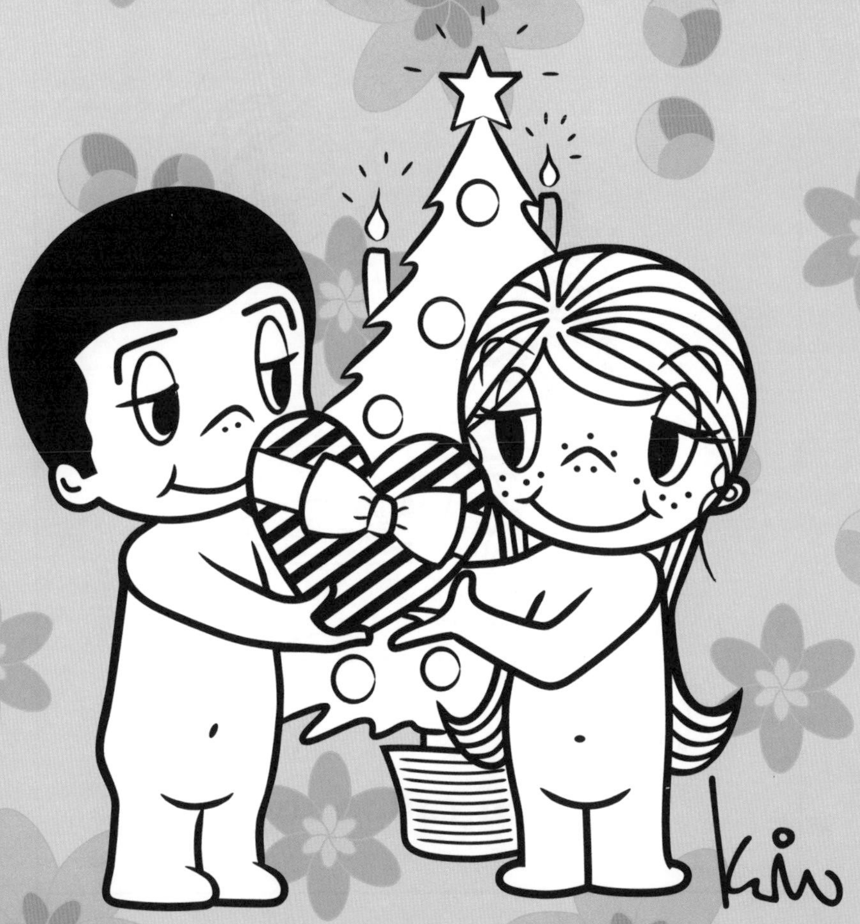

love is...

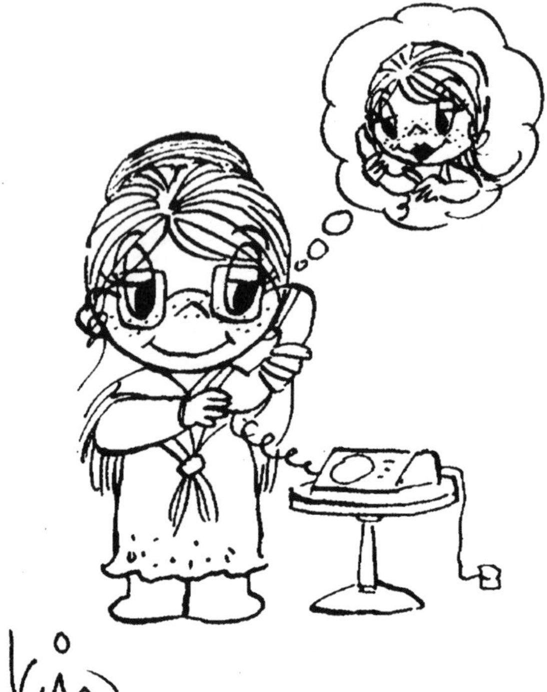

...a call to say "hello"

love is...

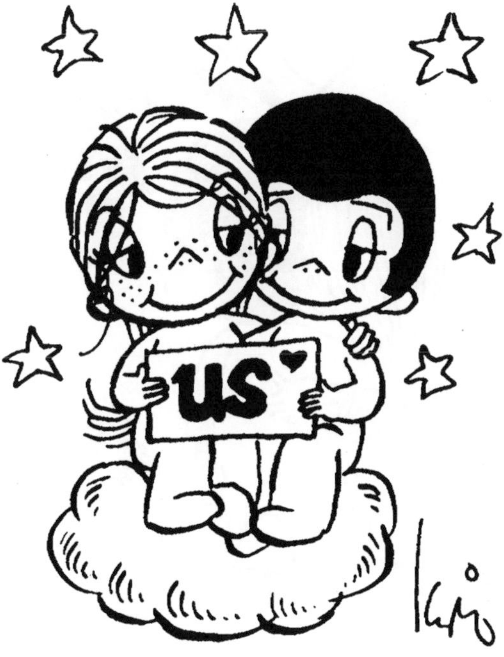
US

...joining forces

love is...

...walking the dog together

love is...

...discussing the number of
children you want

love is...

...parenthood

love is...

...giving them all your love
and attention

love is...

...being together,
wherever you are

love is...

...caring

love is...

...a reassuring hand

love is...

...the way to encourage him

love is...

...getting your act together

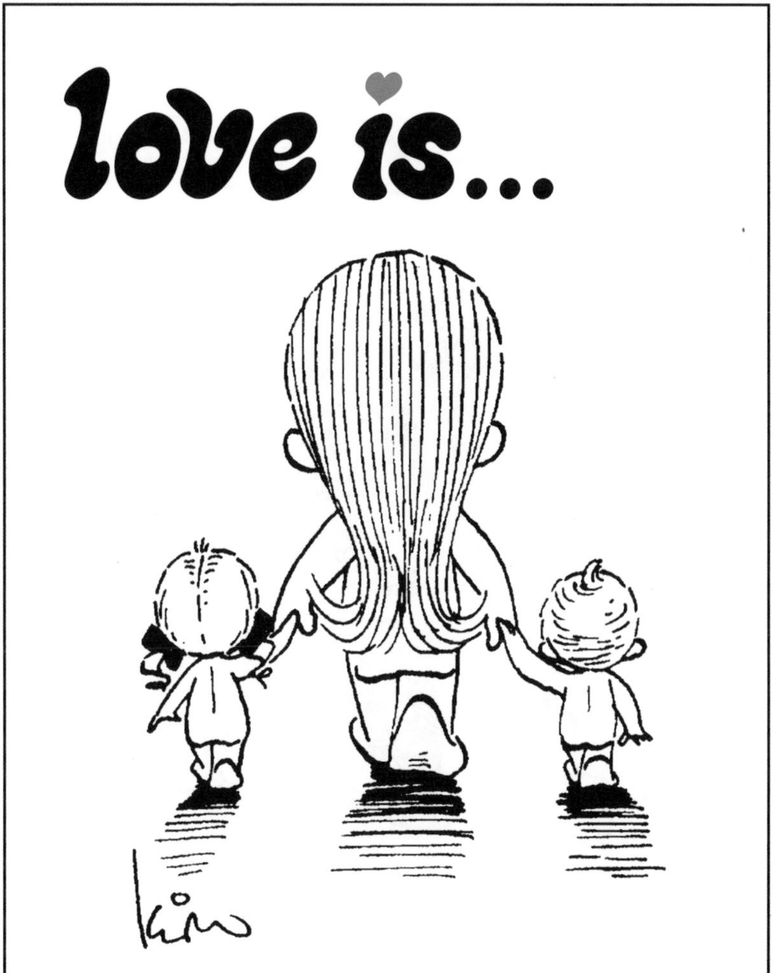
love is...
...holding hands

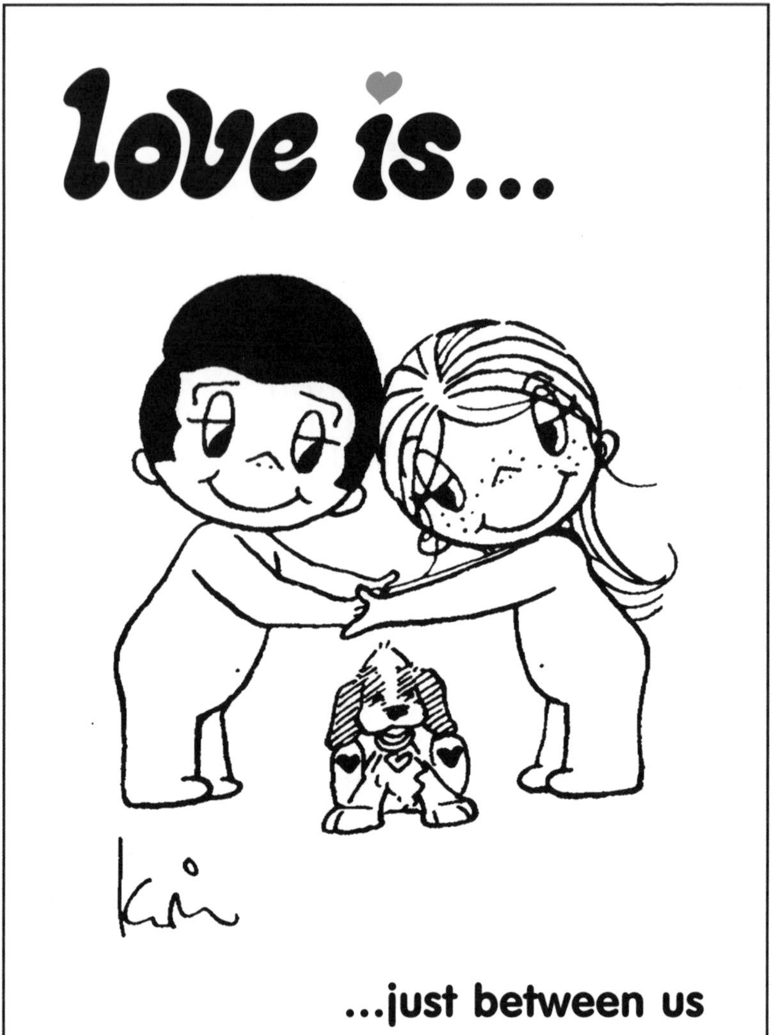
love is...
...just between us

love is...

...a happy childhood

love is...

...a log cabin, a sunset, and you

love is...

...making pancakes on
Saturday morning

love is...

...why I write to you so often

love is...

...someone to carry you home
after a long day

...someone to take care of you

love is...

...keeping a light in the
window for him

love is...

...sitting on the back porch
with Grandpa

love is...

...decorating your first
apartment together

love is...

...your recipe for harmony
at home

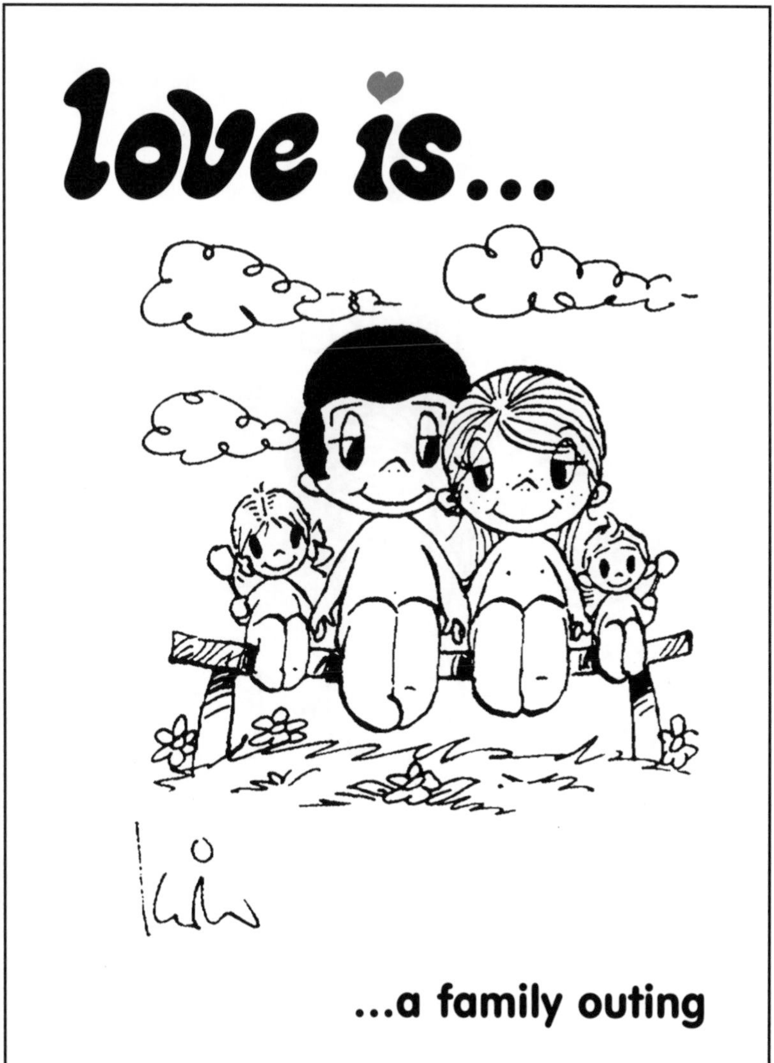
love is...
...a family outing

...taking her little brother on your movie date

love is...

...doing things as a family

love is...

...inviting her to family
gatherings

love is...

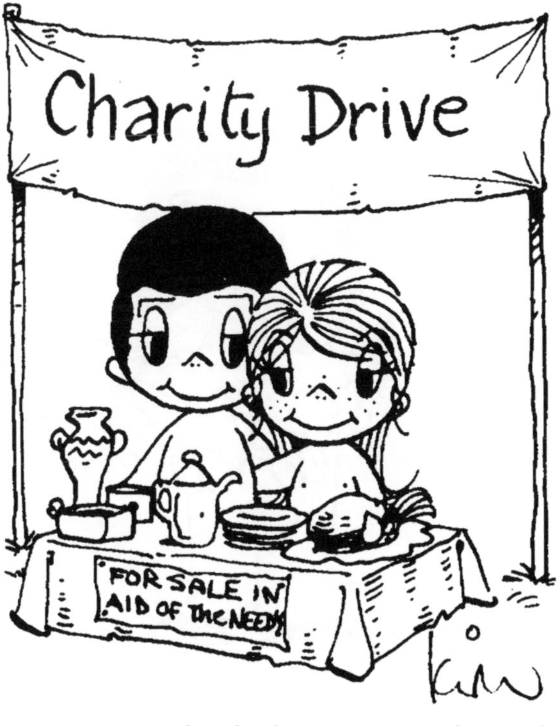
Charity Drive
FOR SALE IN
AID OF THE NEEDY

...helping people who help people

love is...

...not being afraid to
show affection

love is...

**...when they remember
Mother's Day**

love is...

...watching your language
when the children are present

love is...

...something that comes in all shapes and sizes

love is...

...helping hands

love is...

...teaching them respect
for nature

love is...

...a family camping trip

love is...

...having someone run to greet you

love is...

...someone to bring you your
favorite slippers

love is...

...someone to wipe your nose

love is...

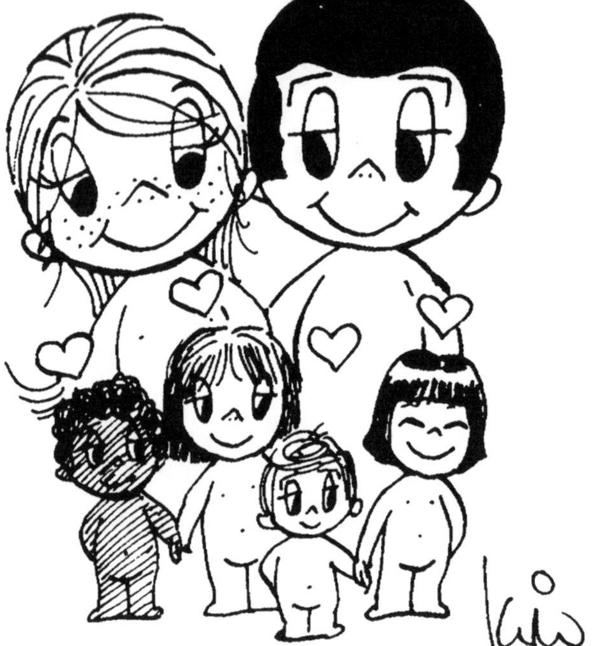

...for everyone

love is...

...seeing your child do well

love is...

...not fun without him

love is...

...sharing your dreams

love is...

...sharing cool treats with
warm hearts

love is...

...being together by
the campfire

love is...

...someone at your feet

love is...

...learning to change a diaper

love is...

...shared pleasures

love is...

...keeping each other company
along life's highways

love is...

...seeing the New Year in
together

love is...

...feeling tiny fingers
touch yours

love is...

...watching for the first
snowflakes of winter

love is...

...sharing with your son the
things you did as a kid

love is...

...letting him into your bed in the morning

love is...

...growing rich with years together

love is...

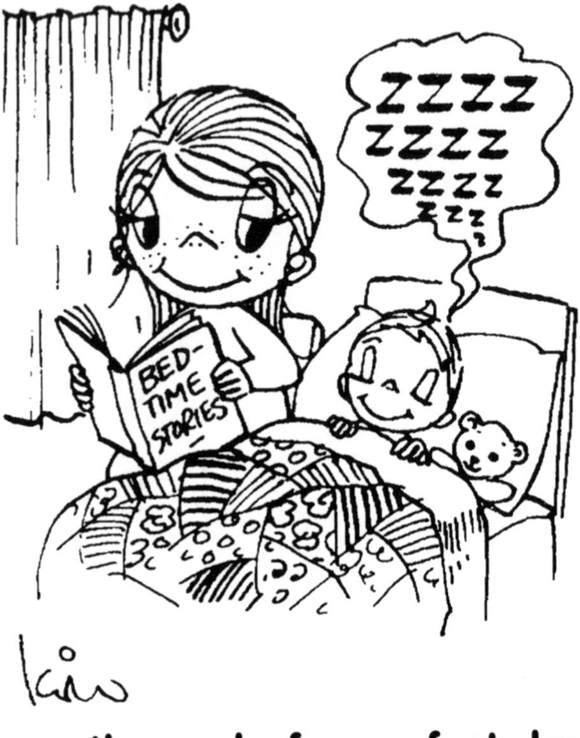
ZZZZ
ZZZZ
ZZZZ
ZZZ
BED-
TIME
STORIES
kim

...the end of a perfect day

love is...

... ups and downs

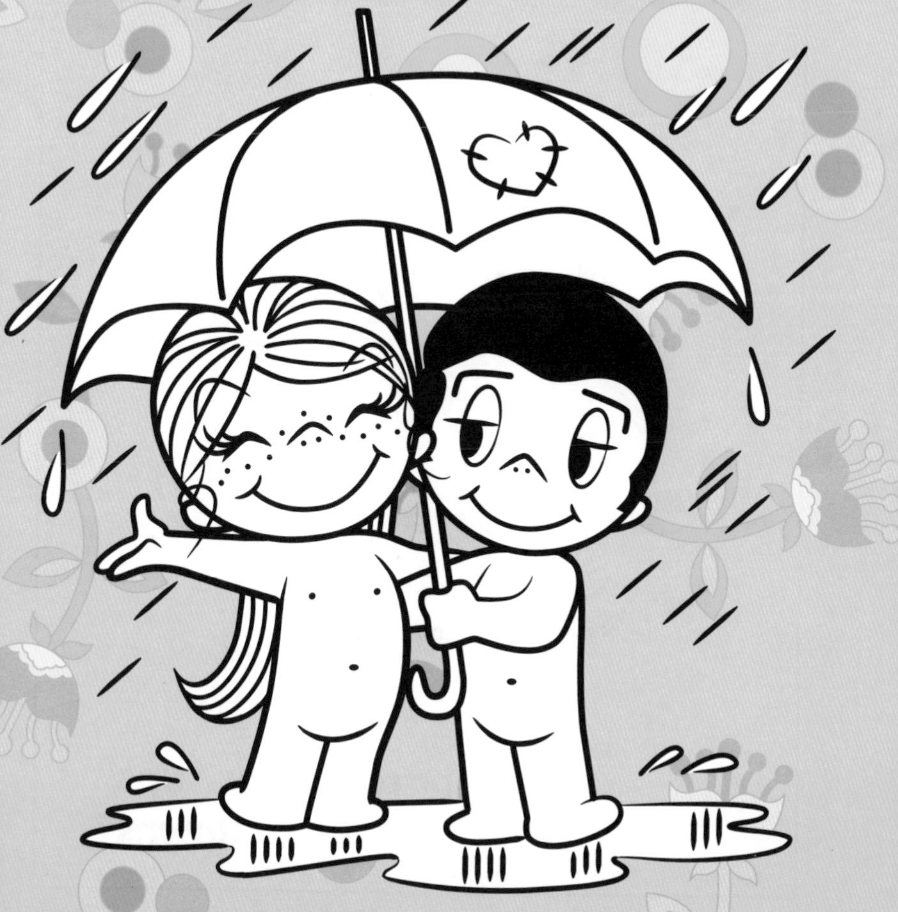

love is...

...sharing your "ups" and "downs"

love is...

...not leading each other
up the garden path

love is...

...being out of sight but not out of mind

love is...

**...when every cloud has
a silver lining**

love is...

...when nothing stops him
from coming to see you

love is...

...sometimes an impossible situation

love is...

...sometimes having heartache

...when he's the best medicine

love is...

...sometimes hard to capture

...being willing to compromise

love is...

...a nice kind of ache

love is...

...trying to see eye to eye

love is...

...finding the right words to say

love is...

...a house full of happiness

love is...

...putting up with his
occasional stubble

...knowing when to leave
him alone

love is...

...feeling good all over

...sometimes a weighty problem

love is...

...not without a few heartaches along the way

love is...

...a puzzle

love is...

...keeping your sense of humor

love is...

...blowing up a storm
of emotion

love is...

...when teardrops sometimes fall like raindrops

love is...

...when the good moments outweigh the bad

love is...

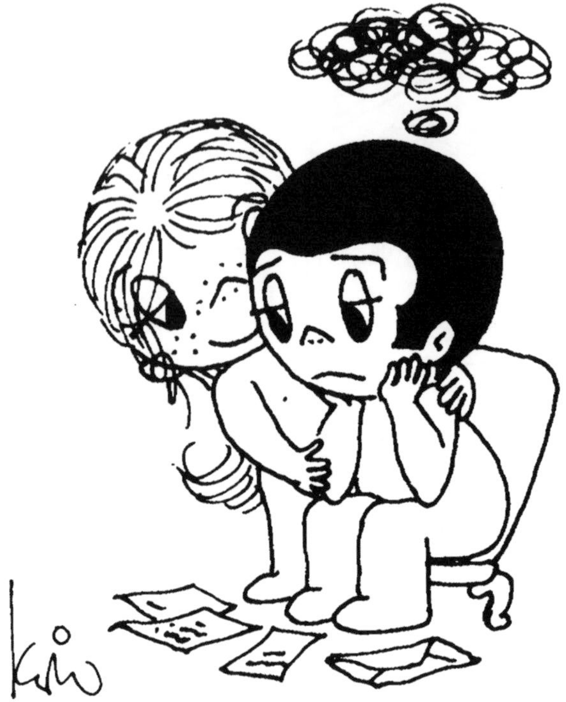

...caring about his problems

love is...

...calling to say "sorry"

love is...

...not putting his faults under a
magnifying glass

love is...

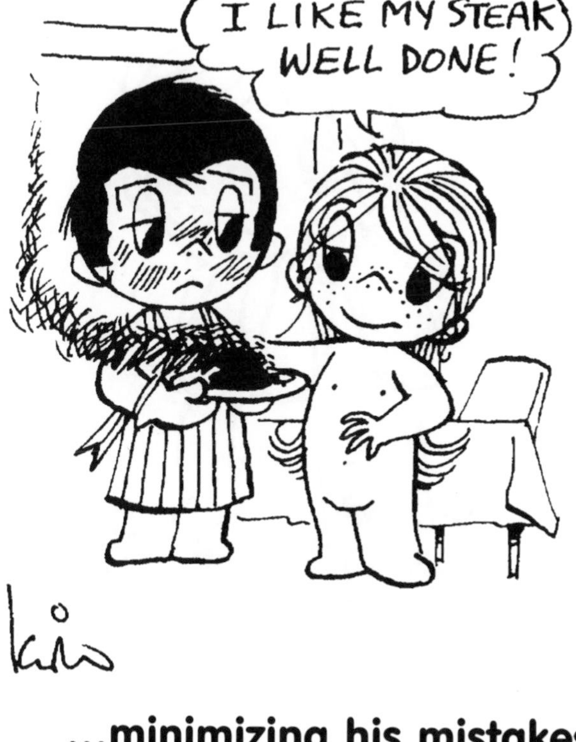
I LIKE MY STEAK WELL DONE!

...minimizing his mistakes

love is...

...fragile

love is...

...not trampling all over
his feelings

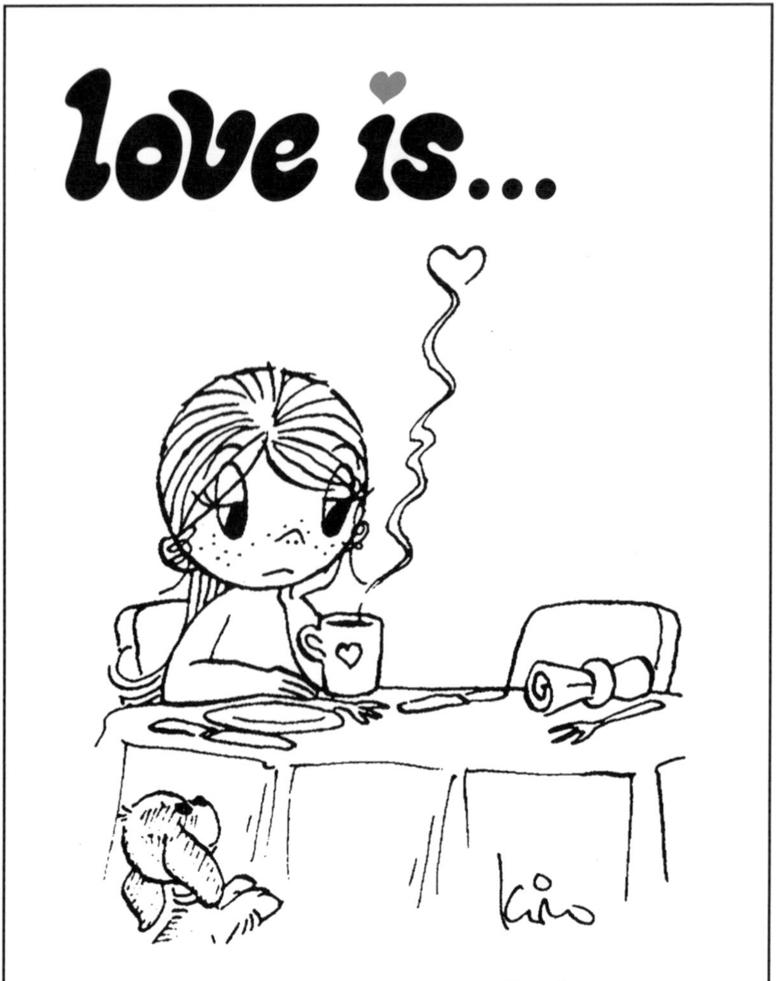
love is...
...missing you

love is...

...sometimes a minefield

love is...

...giving each other emotional support

love is...

...backing each other up

love is...

...holding your new baby

love is...

...what chases away the dark clouds

love is...

...sharing the happiest day of your life

love is...

...willing him to call you

love is...

...sometimes getting into
a pickle

love is...

...the way to ease the stress of everyday life

love is...

...being the first to say "sorry"

love is...

...a basketful of surprises

love is...

...when you'd rather fight than
lose him

love is...

...knowing a hug can bridge
an impasse

love is...

...mending a bruised heart

love is...

...worth all the heartache

love is...

...sometimes having to mask
your emotions

love is...

...taking your chances

love is...

...sometimes just you and a
"blue moon"

love is...

...understanding each other's
weaknesses

love is...

...knowing when to call
a cease fire

love is...

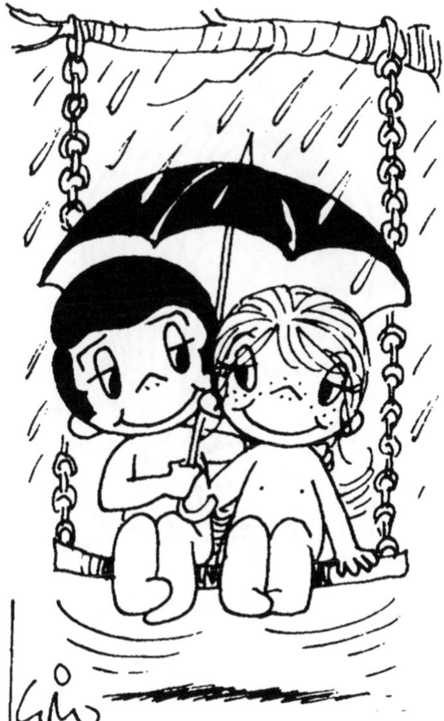

...swinging in the rain

love is...

...making up

love is...

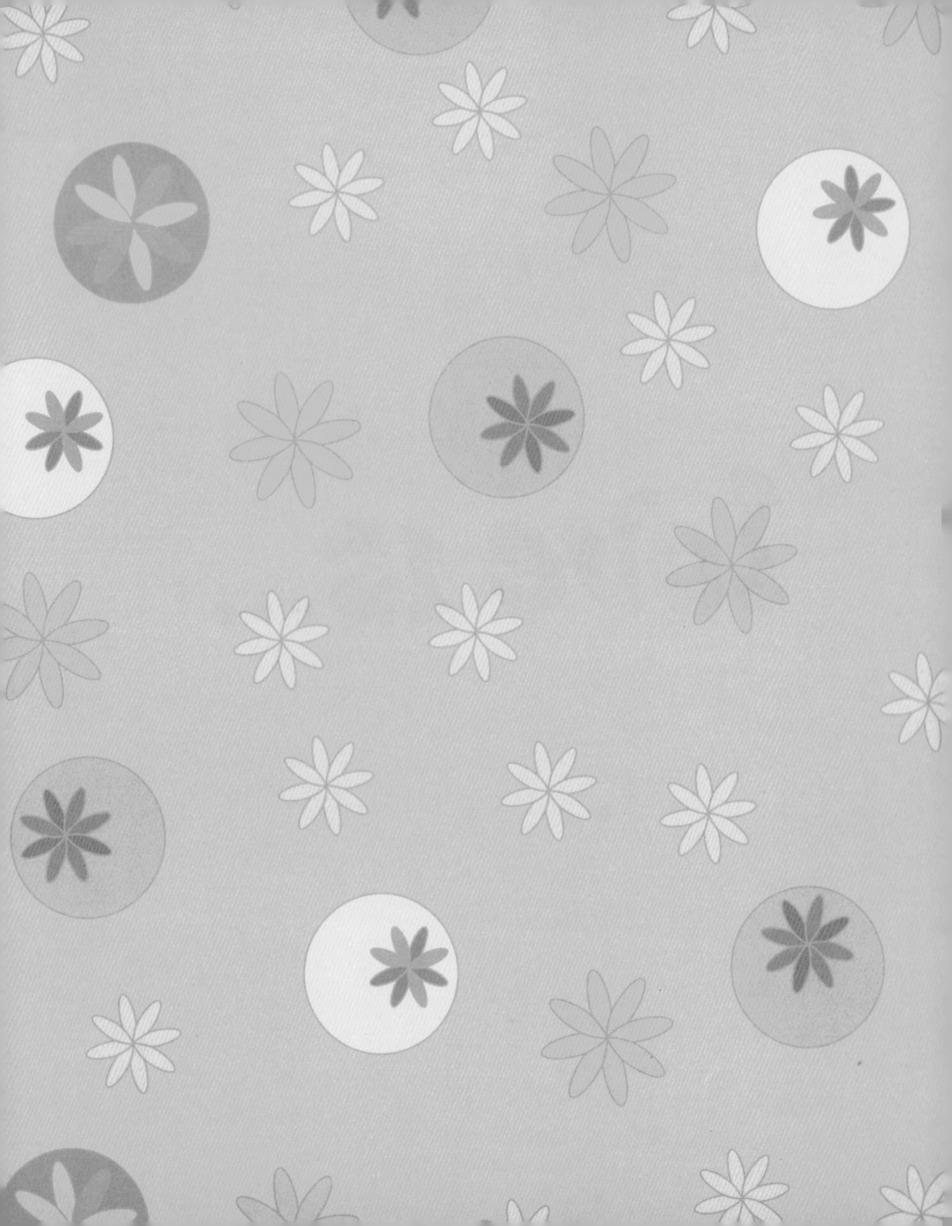

. . . sugar and spice

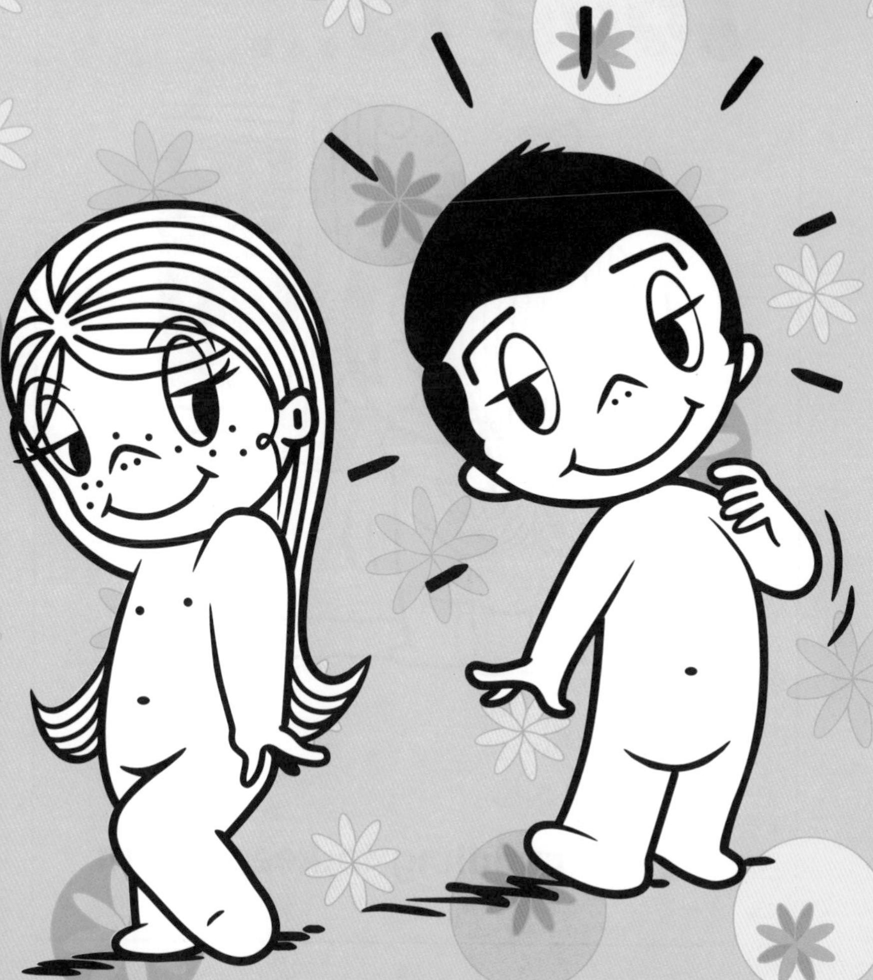

love is...

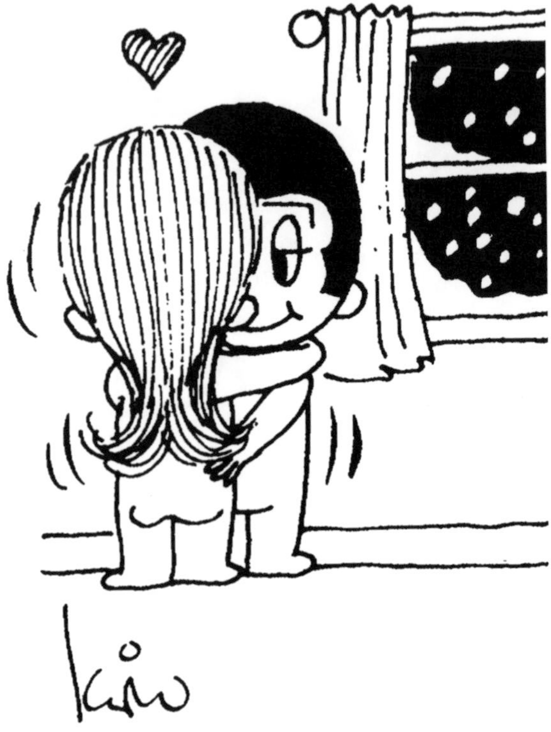

...cuddling to keep warm

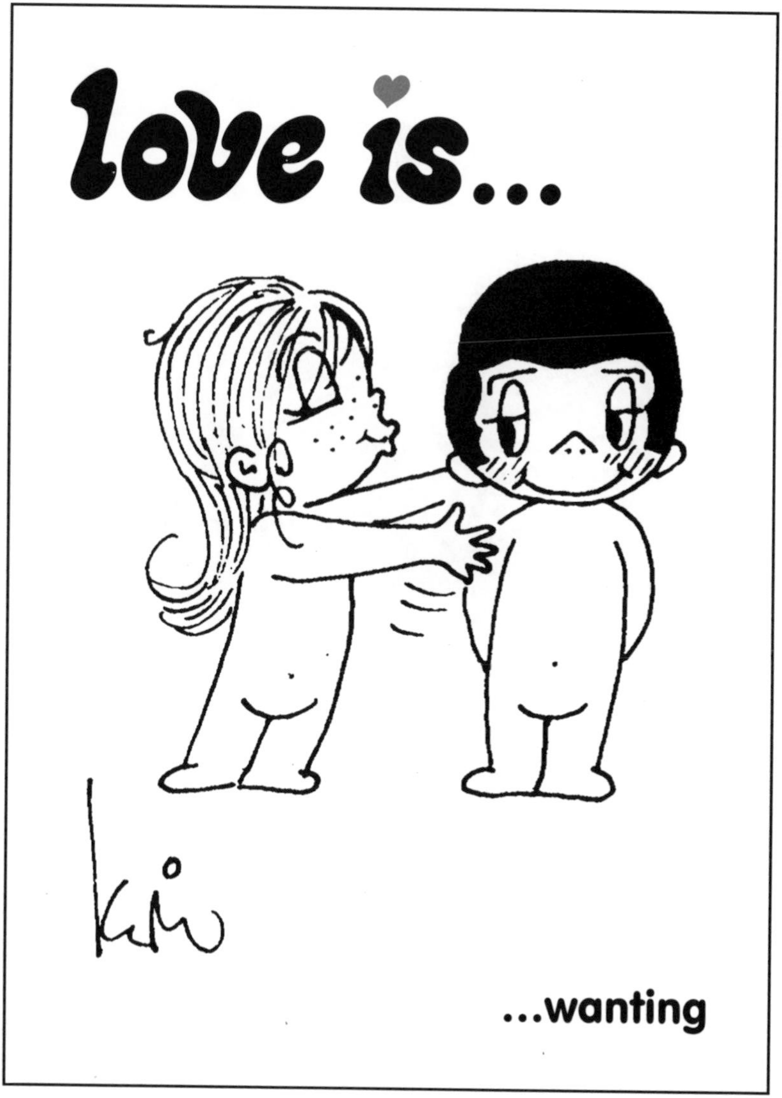
love is...
...wanting

love is...

...warming her nose

love is...

...remembering his strong arms

love is...

...finding he has a high "kissability" factor

love is...

...getting ready to give him some "lip"

love is...

...nibbling her ear

love is...

...someone to share long
winter evenings with

love is...

...blowing away the cobwebs

love is...

...better than socks in bed

love is...

...a little bit of fantasy

love is...

...when she casts a spell
over you

love is...

...hoping he'll make a pass at you

love is...

...getting all sentimental
over him

love is...

...wearing something that turns his head

love is...

...steaming up his glasses

love is...

...when his intentions are
strictly romantic

love is...

...telling her she was the prettiest girl at the party

love is...

...slinking up to him in
something black

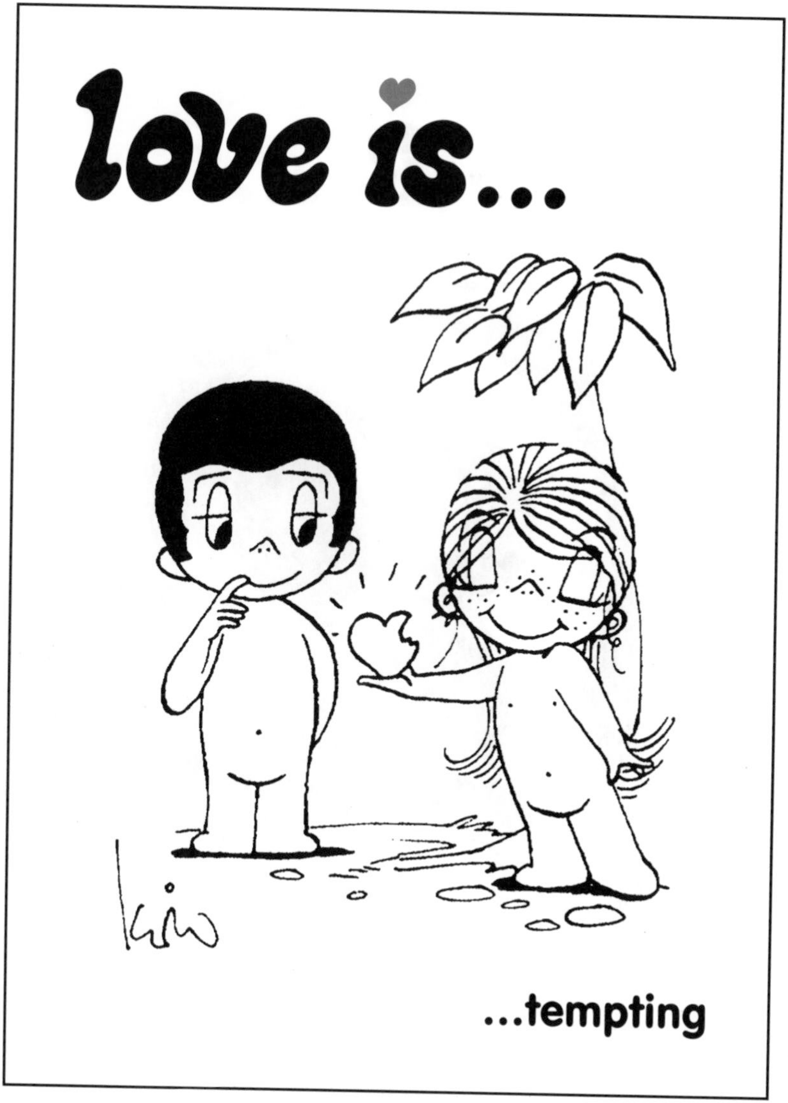
love is...
...tempting

love is...

...being oblivious to the outside world

love is...

...great for your circulation

love is...

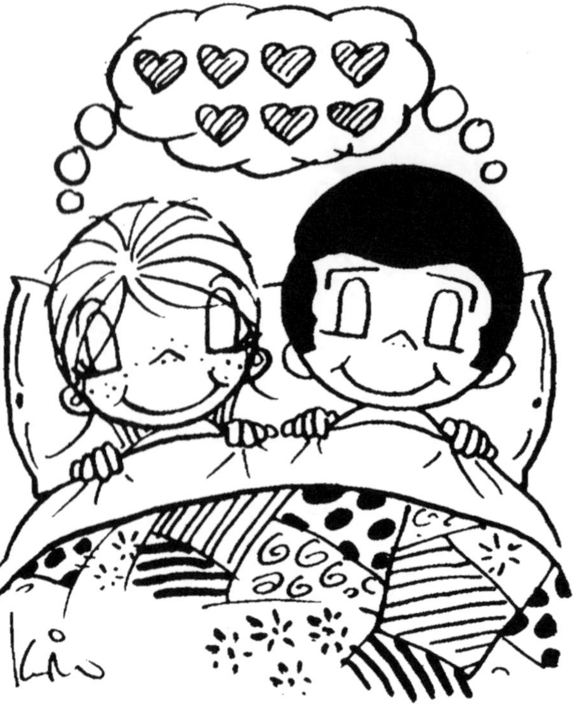

...dreaming the same dream

...doing that to me "one more time"

love is...

...just the two of us

love is...

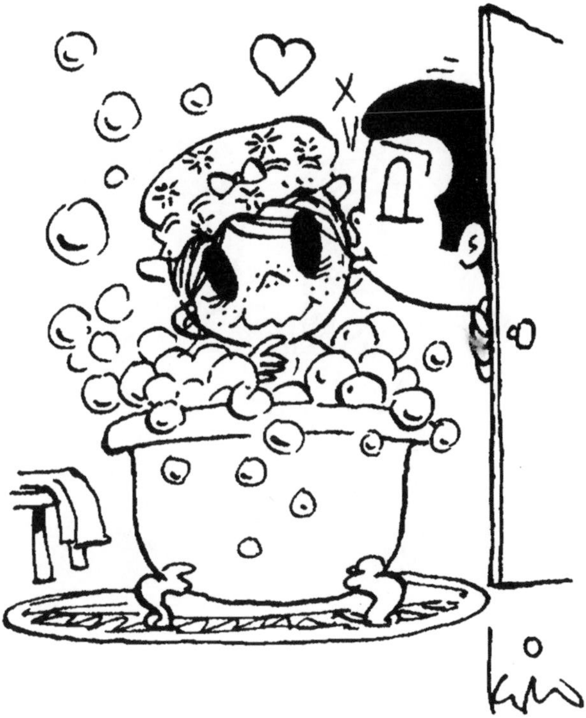

X
V

...a surprise kiss

love is...

...playing footsie

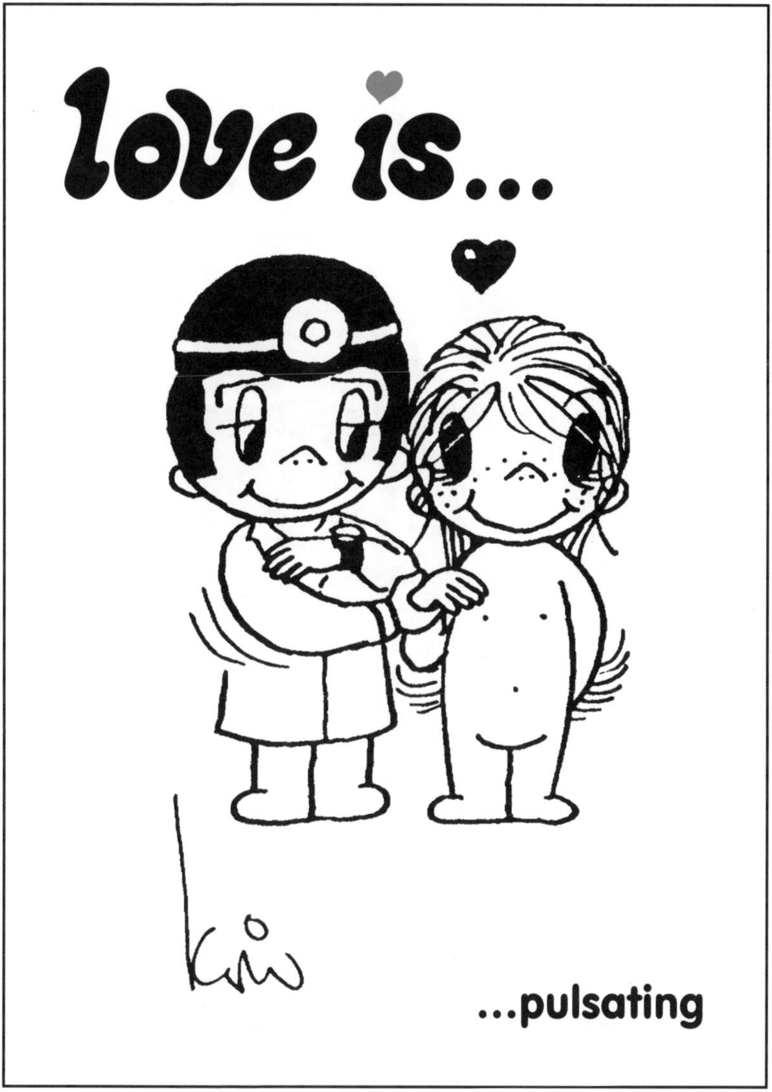
love is...
...pulsating

love is...

...making the most of short
days and long winter nights

love is...

...making hay together

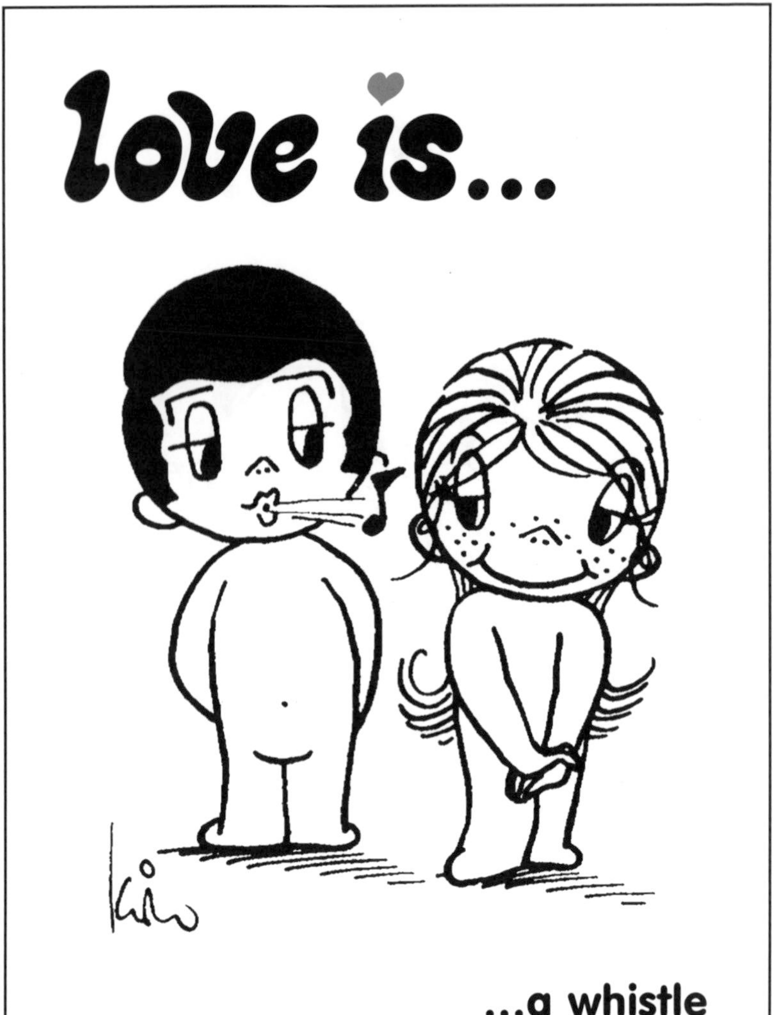
love is...
Kim
...a whistle

...massaging away her backache

love is...

...a double sleeping bag

love is...

...keeping up the romance
after marriage

love is...

...taking your eyes off the ball

love is...

...knowing what he wants for
his birthday

love is...

...giving him the boot

love is...

...lots of long, lingering kisses

love is...

...still getting that old feeling

love is...

...sleeping with a smile on your face

love is...

...giving him encouragement

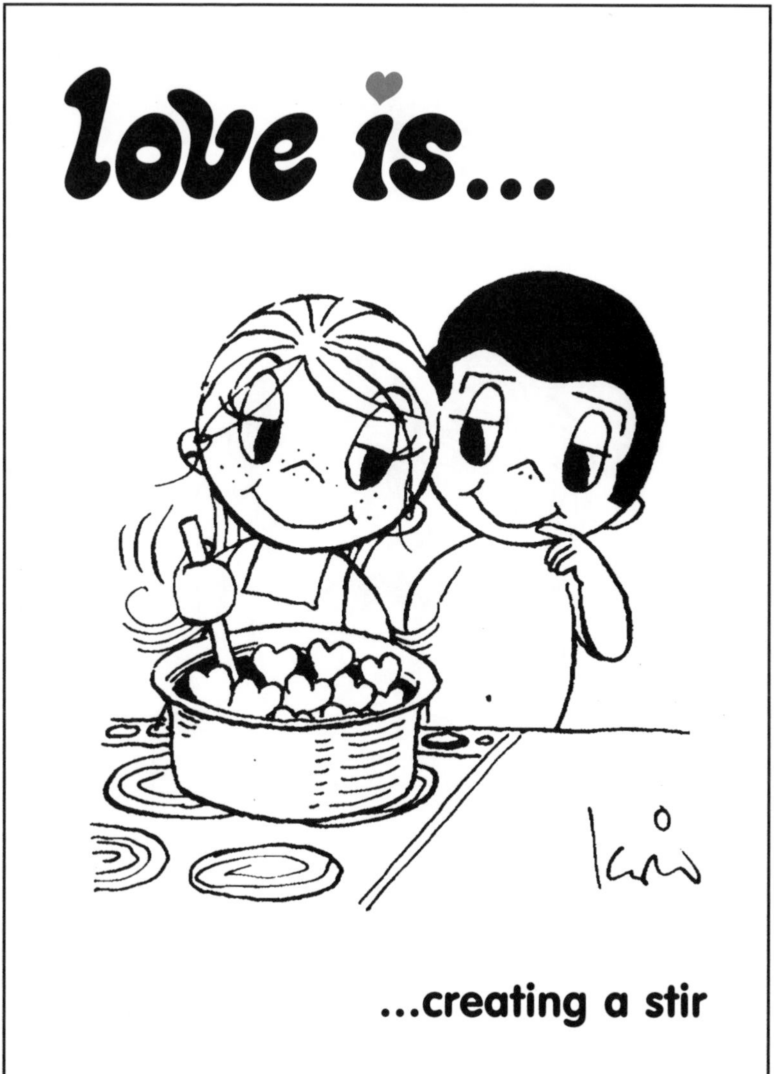
love is...
...creating a stir

love is...

...helped by a little candlelight

love is...

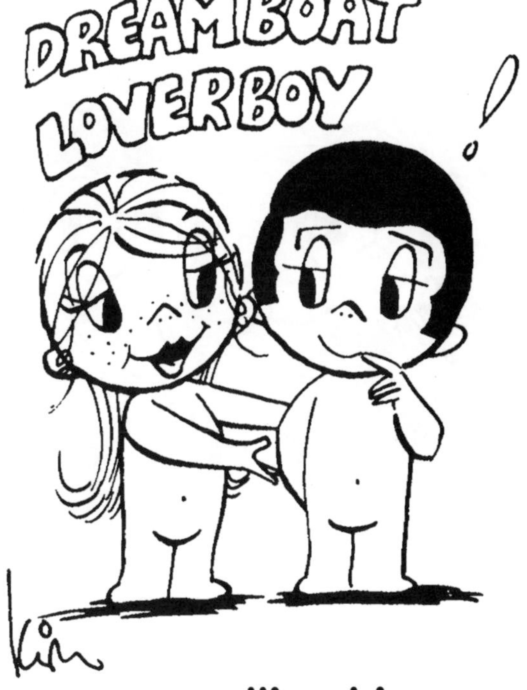
DREAMBOAT
LOVERBOY

...calling him names

...an evening of champagne and roses

love is...

...knowing you're in safe hands

...taking the phone off the hook

...when the temperature's rising

love is...

...getting a tingle when he
gives you "the look"

love is...

...dusting that crumb from his chin

love is...

...finding the park bench
where you first met

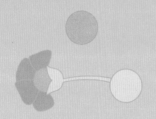

love is...

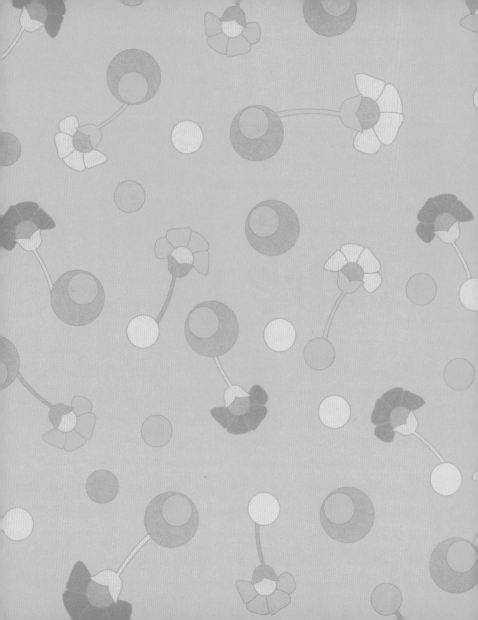

. . . all this and more

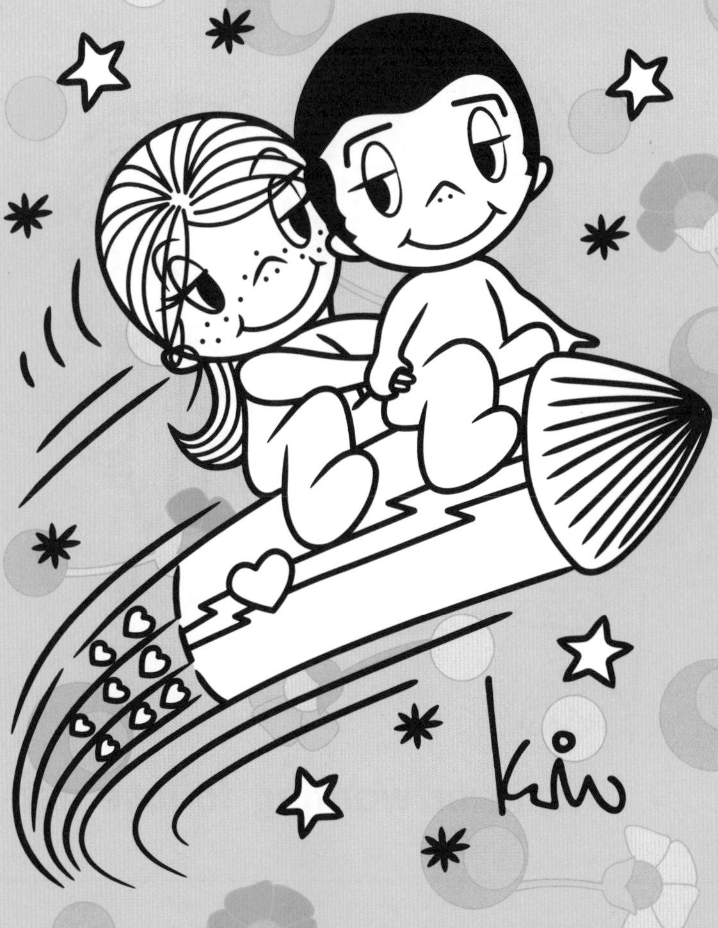
kim

love is...

...never wanting to lose her

love is...

...throwing away all those other addresses

love is...

...pinching yourself to make
sure it's for real

...seeing your future in the stars

love is...

...feeling her heartbeat forever

love is...

...knowing it's the real thing

love is...

...falling in love all over again

love is...

...when you can't think of anyone else

love is...

...two hearts beating as one

love is...

...his favorite shade of lipstick

love is...

...not having to face the new
day alone

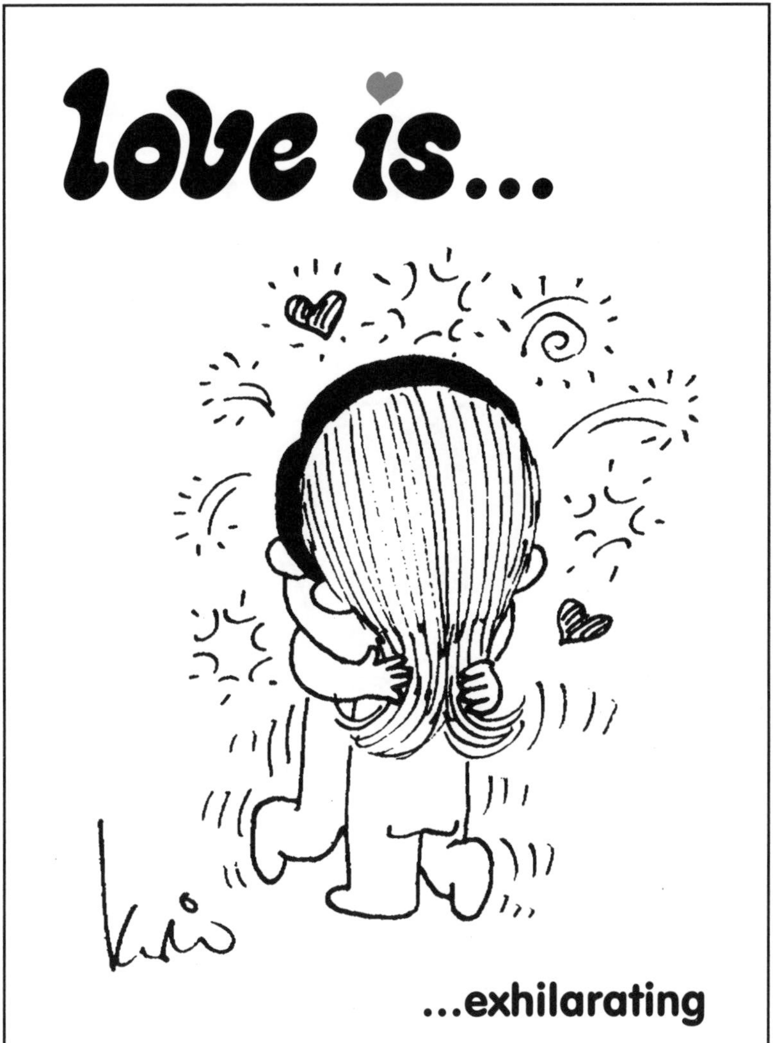
love is...
...exhilarating

love is...

...wishing time would stand still

love is...

...seeing his face everywhere

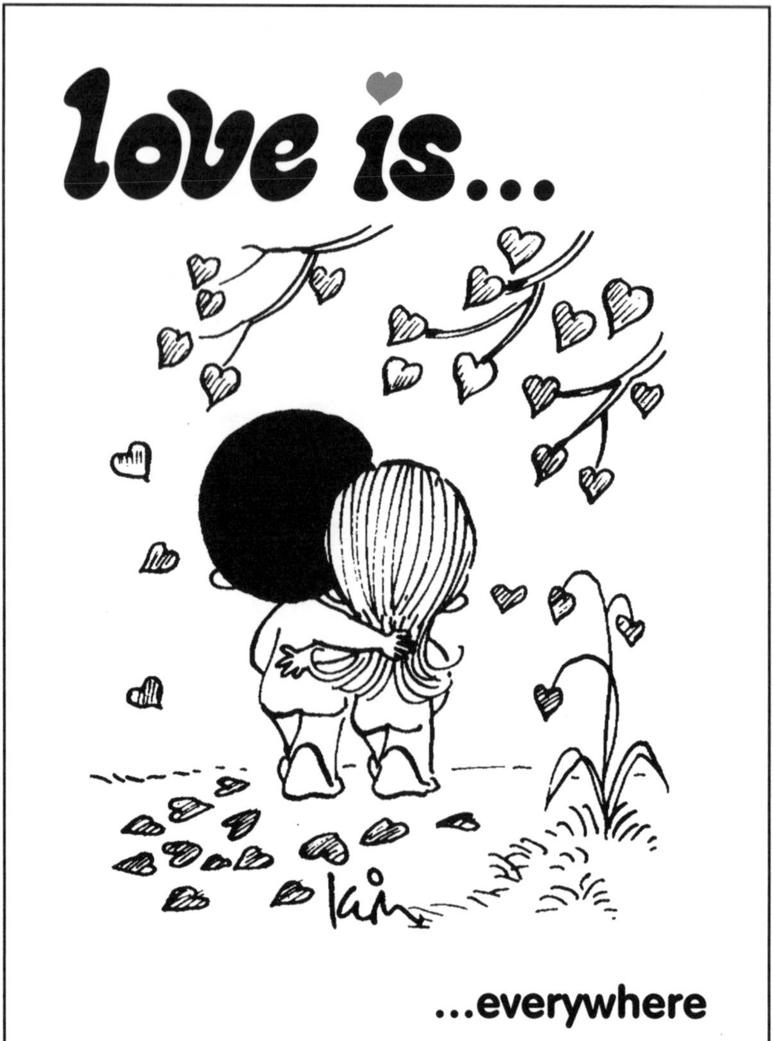
love is...
...everywhere

love is...

...reading each other's thoughts

love is...

...the greatest gift of all

love is...

...the universal language

love is...

...the pathway to happiness

love is...

...a field of dreams

love is...

...just you and me

love is...

...being hooked only on you

love is...

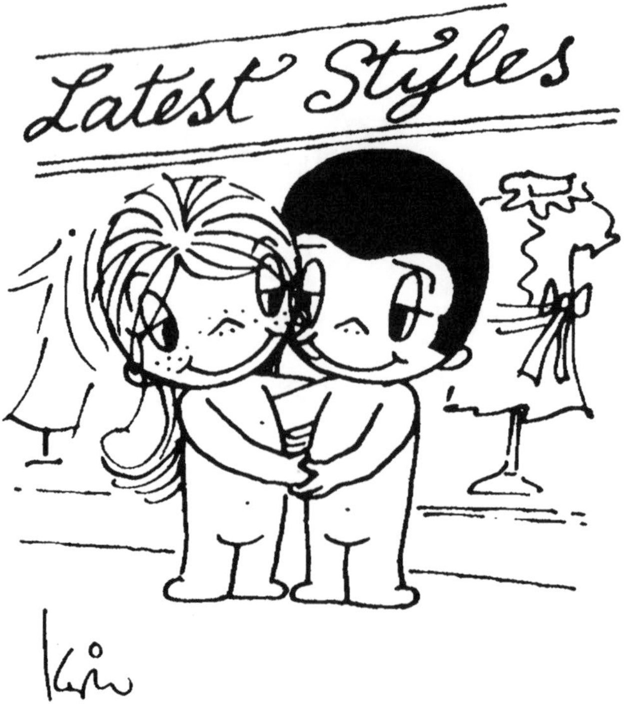
Latest Styles

...never out of fashion

love is...

...plotting your future

love is...

...what heaven must be like

love is...

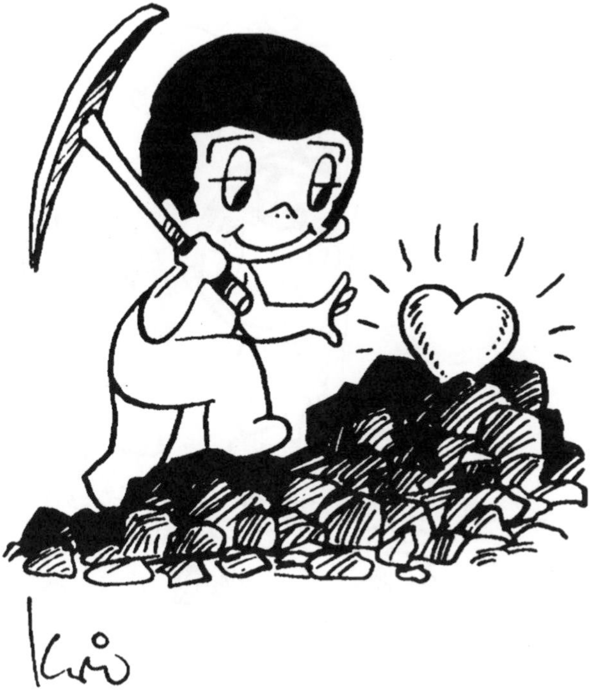

...a “mine” of happiness

love is...

...like sailing into
uncharted waters

...wondering how and why she picked you

...when the hours go like minutes

love is...

...hitting the jackpot

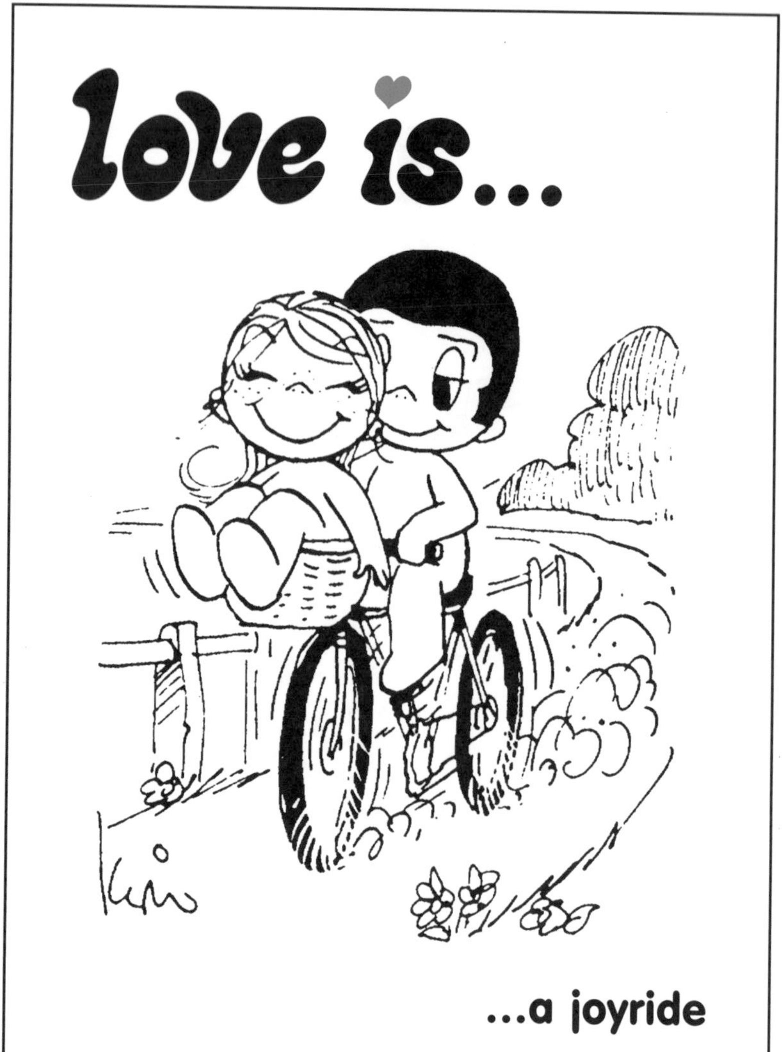
love is...
...a joyride

...enjoying the "sunset years" together

love is...

...a kind of heaven, only better!

love is...

...the catch of a lifetime

love is...

...finding you've got the world
in your arms

love is...

...what makes you feel like jumping for joy

love is...

...when your heart takes flight

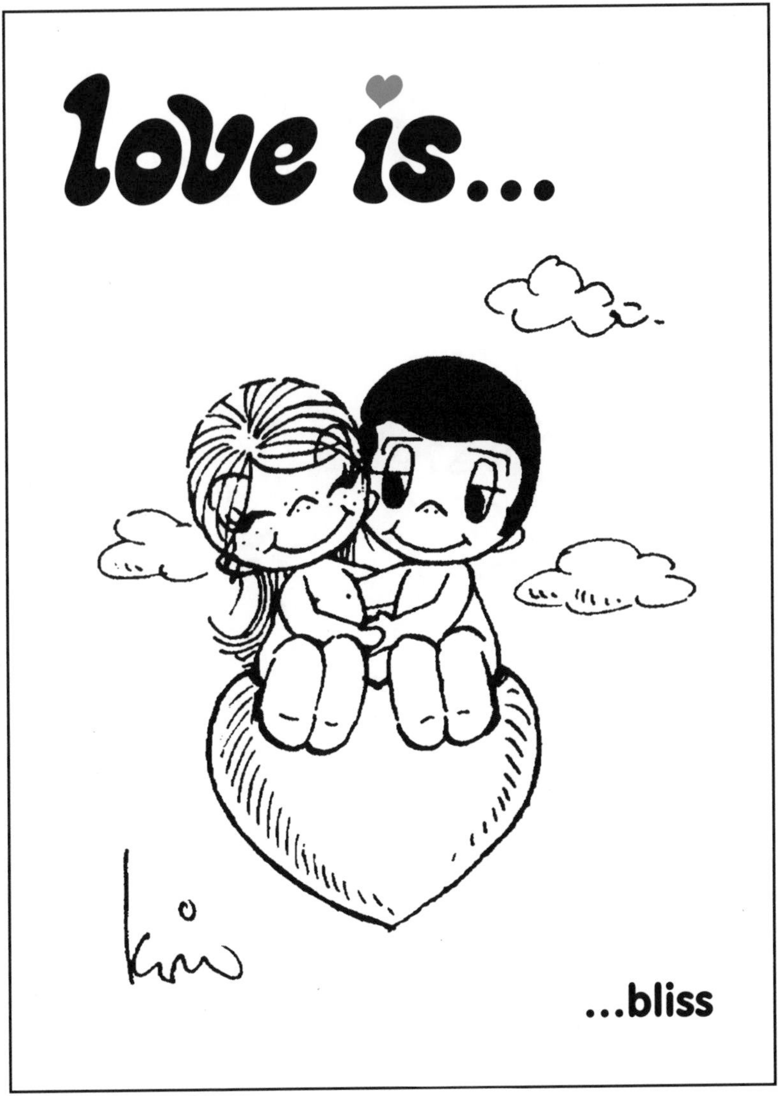
love is...
...bliss

...wondering if she's thinking
what you're thinking

love is...

...two minds with but one thought

love is...

...not letting time run out

love is...

...a flight of fantasy

love is...

...with you, come sunrise and sunset

...putting your brand on him

love is...

**...like discovering
a hidden treasure**

love is...

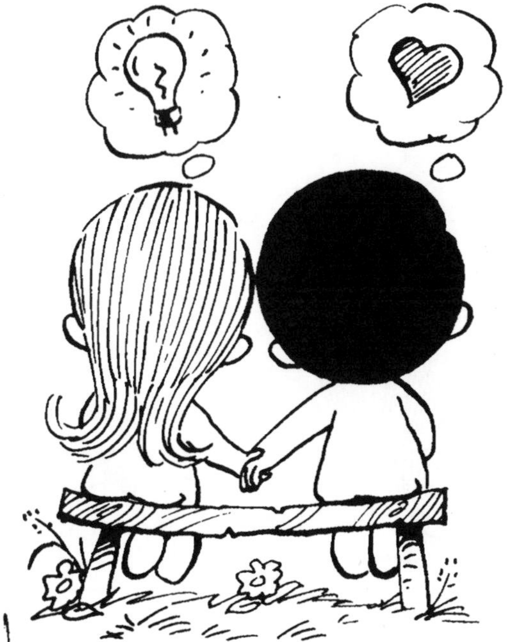

...the brightest idea of all

love is...

...plain for all to see

love is...

...when it's always spring
in your heart

love is...

...finding new horizons together

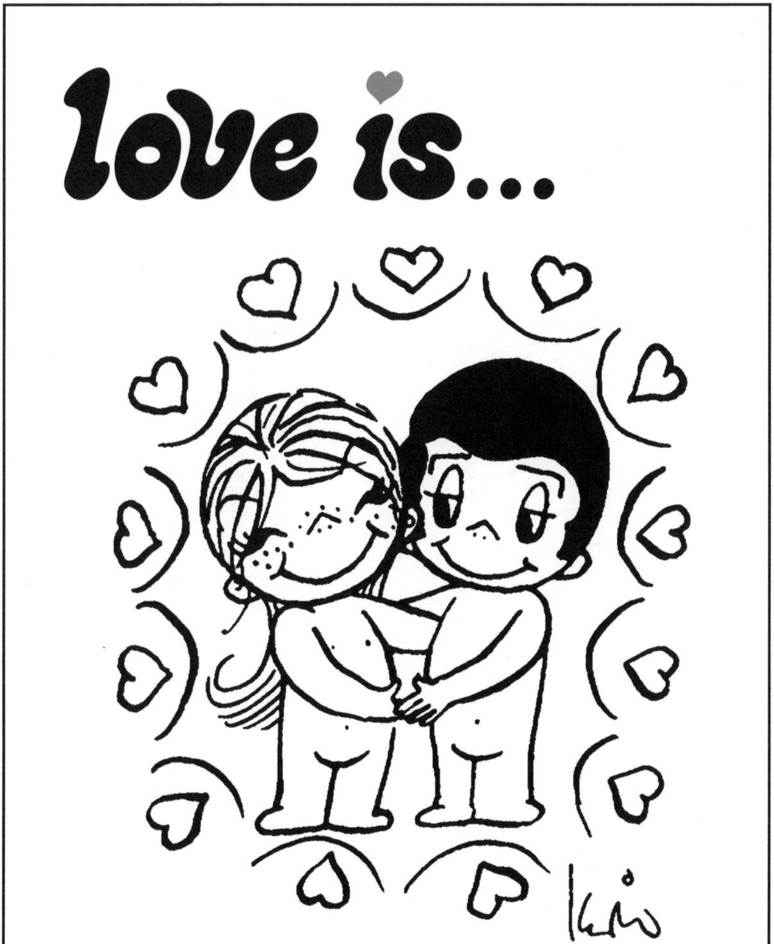
love is...
...all this and more

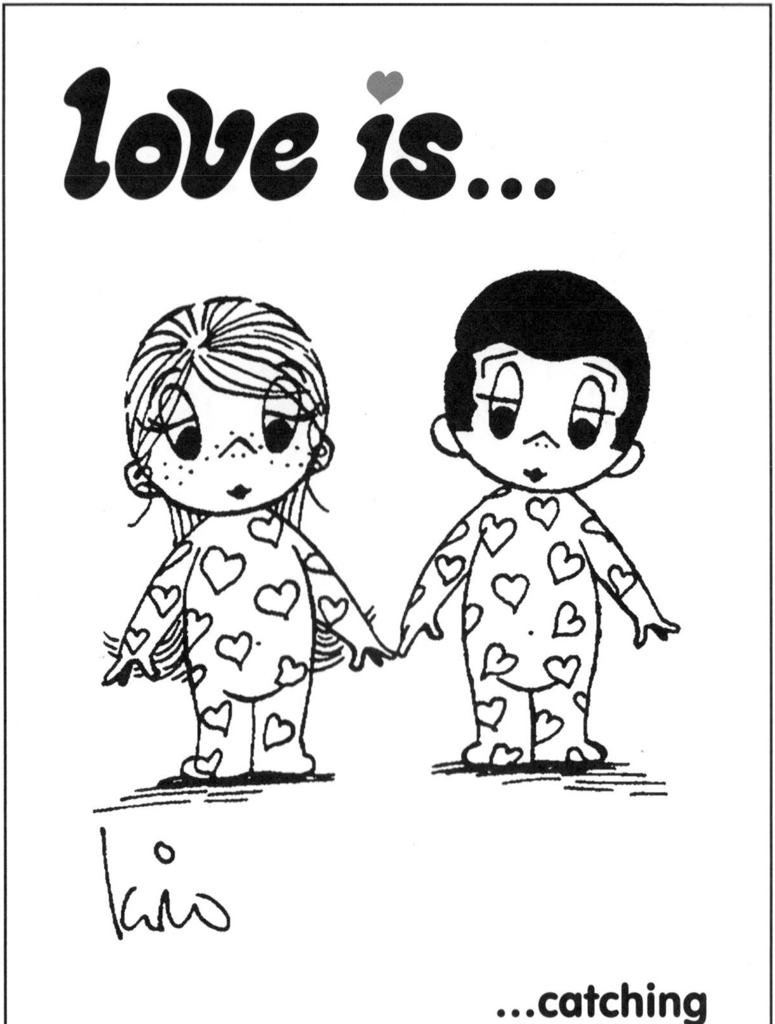
love is...
...catching

love is...

...like the tide,
impossible to stop

love is...

...just being happy to be near you

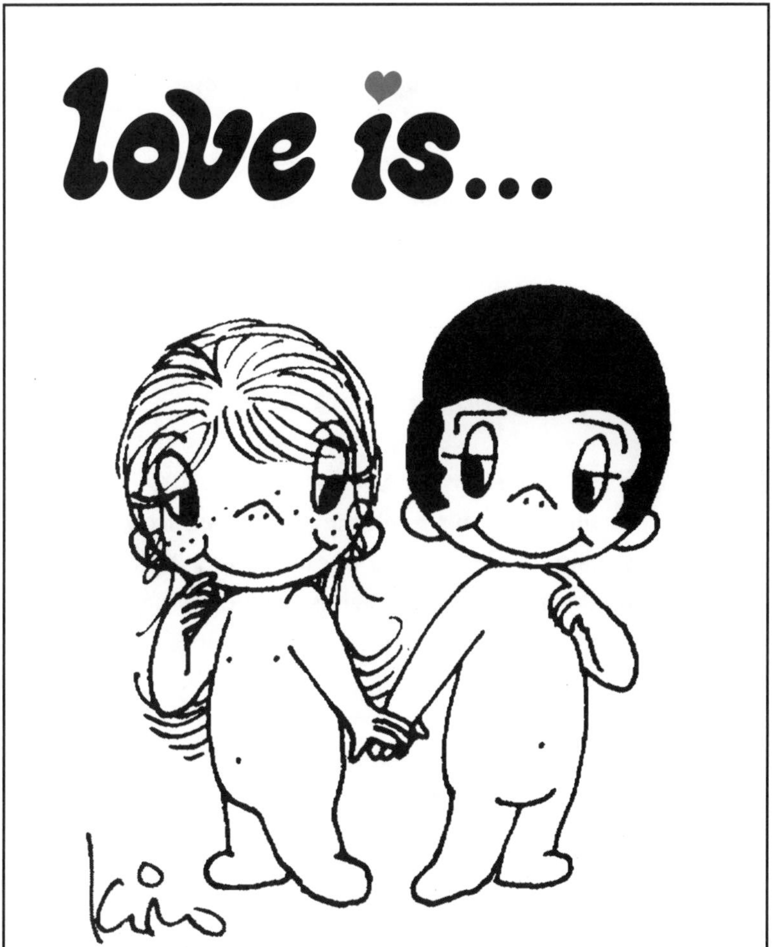
love is...
...just the beginning

Design by Celina Carvalho
Production Manager: Jonathan Lopes

Library of Congress Cataloging-in-Publication Data
has been applied for.
ISBN 13: 978-0-8109-5791-6
ISBN 10: 0-8109-5791-4

Printed and bound in China
10 9 8 7 6 5 4 3

HNA ▮▮▮▮▮
harry n. abrams, inc.
a subsidiary of La Martinière Groupe
115 West 18th Street
New York, NY 10011
www.hnabooks.com